What Am I Supposed to Do with My Life?

GOD'S WILL DEMYSTIFIED

JOHNNIE MOORE

W Publishing Group

An Imprint of Thomas Nelson

Published in Nashville, Tennessee, by W Publishing, an imprint of Thomas Nelson.

Published in association with Yates & Yates, www.yates2.com.

Thomas Nelson, Inc., titles may be purchased in bulk for educational, business, fund-raising, or sales promotional use. For information, please e-mail SpecialMarkets@ThomasNelson.com.

Any Internet addresses, phone numbers, or company or product information printed in this book are offered as a resource and are not intended in any way to be or to imply an endorsement by Thomas Nelson, nor does Thomas Nelson vouch for the existence, content, or services of these sites, phone numbers, companies, or products beyond the life of this book.

Scripture quotations are taken from the following translations: (ESV) THE ENGLISH STANDARD VERSION. © 2001 by Crossway Bibles, a division of Good News Publishers; (HCSB) HOLMAN CHRISTIAN STANDARD BIBLE. © 1999, 2000, 2002, 2003 by Broadman and Holman Publishers. All rights reserved; (KJV) King James Version of the Bible. Public domain; (NASB) NEW AMERICAN STANDARD BIBLE®, © The Lockman Foundation 1960, 1962, 1963, 1968, 1971, 1972, 1973, 1975, 1977, 1995. Used by permission; (NIV) HOLY BIBLE: NEW INTERNATIONAL VERSION®. © 1973, 1978, 1984 by International Bible Society. Used by permission of Zondervan Publishing House. All rights reserved; (NKJV) THE NEW KING JAMES VERSION. © 1982 by Thomas Nelson, Inc. Used by permission. All rights reserved.

Library of Congress Control Number: 2014942539

ISBN 978-0-8499-6452-7

Printed in the United States of America

14 15 16 17 18 19 RRD 6 5 4 3 2 1

Meu querido filho, Edward:

This book is dedicated to you.

*I wrote it for you, hoping it will be a guide
for life that you will cherish one day,*

*You have brought us joy and happiness
we didn't even know existed,*

*You made us love in a way we didn't
even know was possible,*

You made us pray like we never have before,

We believe in you,

We love you.

Te amo muito,

Papai

"Your word is a lamp for my feet, a light on my path."

PSALM 119:105 NIV

CONTENTS

Contents

CONTENTS

INTRODUCTION

FOR NEARLY TWO THOUSAND YEARS TOO MANY Christians have embraced a lie. The lie is cast in spiritual tones and therefore seems, on the surface, innocent enough.

Yet it's a lie so deceptive that even the most pious believe it without knowing it, and its widespread practice has robbed the world of a thousand kinds of good that would have been hers had Christianity followed God's original path.

It's a lie so clandestine that it has woven its way in and out of Christian history nearly undetected.

It's a lie so sinister that it has robbed millions of people of their souls.

This book has been written to expose this lie once and for all and to call a new generation of Christians to send the lie to hell—where it belongs.

What is The Lie?

It is that God's will is hard to find.

It isn't.

PART ONE

HOW CAN I FIND GOD'S WILL FOR MY LIFE?

ONE

KNOCKING GOD IN THE CHOPS

Your will is at constant war with God's

I'VE NEVER SEEN STUDENTS UNDER MORE STRESS THAN when they are trying to find God's will for their lives. After more than a dozen years in higher education, I can spot a kid stressing over this question a mile away.

They look as if they've fallen off the back of a truck. They're dazed. They have puffy eyes and they stare out into space as if trying to make sense of a mirage in the desert.

They are traumatized by the ups and downs of answering life's question of purpose, and they feel an extraordinary amount of pressure not to "miss God's will," as if God's will is a bull's-eye that they have to hit or spend the rest of their lives suffering for missing it.

The problem is that life isn't so simple. Life is *filled* with ambiguous situations and questions that don't have clear answers. Questions about what career to choose, where to live, and who to marry are all piled up in the middle of life's roadways. And it seems as if there are often moments in life when you're standing at a crossroads where either path seems to be a good one, and you're vexed by the choice that God would have you make.

Instead of making a decision in one direction and sticking with it, many get a case of decision paralysis and give up altogether. They start roaming around, hoping God will drop a blinking sign out of the sky with an arrow as big as the truck they fell off, saying, "Go here!" "Marry her!" "Do that!"

WHY IS IT THIS WAY?

You wouldn't expect it to be this hard, would you?

I mean, you would think that God would make himself clearer when it comes to these types of decisions and questions. After all, the consequences are significant. Most of the folks I know who are asking questions about the will of God for their lives are genuinely good people who genuinely want to please God. So why wouldn't God just say, "Here's the way to go . . . here's the place to live . . . here's the job to take . . . here's the decision to make . . . here's the person to love"? That sure seems a lot easier than having to wade through all the stress required to make basic choices about your future.

Why, instead, does God make us suffer through these grueling decisions with no clear answer and no booming voice from the sky?

Wouldn't it be better for him, for us, and for the world if he made the whole thing a little simpler?

Yet he doesn't.

Every good-hearted, genuine follower of God I know has faced a crossroads in life, one of these extraordinarily difficult decisions. They've stood with exasperated eyes, looking at divergent paths, begging and pleading to know the way.

My friend Elliott is a good example. He is a young leader with an exceptional job in a great company founded and led by Christians. He's been there for a while; he has gained respect and a reputation, and slowly gathered more influence in the organization. He planned on staying there forever, and was happy to do so.

Then, out of the blue, he received a job offer from another fantastic organization. The opportunity offered him the chance to work full-time on his passion to provide clean water and help children in impoverished nations. It was the chance to move from spending some of his time on his passion to investing his entire career in it, but the decision required drastic changes to his life. He would have to move to another city, leave behind the years of progress he had made in his current company, and even work for a reduced salary, which would no longer allow him to give as liberally to charitable organizations as he had in the past.

He prayed, and even fasted. He begged God to show him the way. He was willing to do whatever God wanted. He pleaded with God to make it clear to him whether he should stay or go. With all of his heart he wanted to do what was right, and he was horrified he would make the wrong decision and pay for it for the rest of his life. This process went on for months and, in the end, he decided to stay where he was. To this day he doesn't know if he made the right decision.

Have you ever felt this way? Almost every Christian I know has had this experience. Why is it that God makes it so hard for those who genuinely want his help to get it when making life's great decisions?

Why are these decisions so hard, and how should you deal with them? We are often told to "follow God's will," but what does that look like? What does that mean? If we followed the idea of God's will we get from modern Christian culture, would it look anything like what God actually intended? Even the phrase "following God's will," though among the most popular and frequently used phrases in all of Christianity, seems to be one of the most ambiguous. Everyone is searching for it, but surprisingly few people have told me that they've actually found it.

What does the Bible actually teach us about the will of God, when following his will seems so nebulous and he seems so silent? And how can we be certain that we make the right decisions when God is refusing to answer our questions, leaving us to do it on our own? We all have questions about the choices that are facing us, and where God's will is leading. I want to help you. That's why I've written this book.

LET'S SETTLE ONE THING UP FRONT

While the idea of God's will seems vague and hard to grasp, some things in Christianity aren't so uncertain. There are concrete foundations upon which to build your life—first and foremost of which is the character of God.

Most Christians don't actually doubt the character of God. They might say they do, and they might question his goodness when life throws them a curveball, but even in those moments of great doubt, they still pose their questions about God's goodness to God himself. When life comes crashing down around them, they pray to the same God they're tempted to doubt, and even in saying,

"God, why?" they are repeating their faith in a God to whom they can ask questions—who they even feel compelled to ask. They believe in a God who *can* answer them, even if he doesn't seem to want to. They rely on the fact that God *does* have a plan for their lives, even if he isn't sharing it with them at the moment.

There is no doubt that God has a plan for his people, and understanding God's plan for your life begins with understanding God's character. That's the heart of the whole conversation. It's like what Brother Andrew—who famously smuggled Bibles into Communist nations for decades—described in his book *And God Changed His Mind.* He wrote of the famous moment in the Old Testament when Moses pleads with God to change his plan for Israel, and God concedes. Of that moment, Brother Andrew wrote:

> We know that God is not only the holy, sovereign, eternal King, but He is also our loving Father—fair, just, compassionate, forgiving and true to His Word. We see, too, that God does not want to hurt or destroy His people; He goes to incredible lengths to avoid it, forgiving not just once or twice, but "seventy times seven" before His righteousness finally demands payment of the penalty for sin. Nobody has even been able to say to God, "You didn't give me a chance!" God

always gives us more chances than we deserve to turn from sin and become His friends. . . .

The answer to the question "Who is God?" is the basis of all prayer, because we cannot relate to God in anything but a superficial way until we know who He is.[1]

What is true of prayer is also true of God's will. Understanding God's will begins with the question, "Who is God?" You can't seriously consider the will of God unless you are convinced that God's will is worth submitting to, that God is trustworthy (and so his will for your life must be trustworthy), and that he is looking out for your best interests. You have to be confident that God really is good, that he really is holy, and that he really does love you with a love so deep that it gives his heart pain to see you living your life to any standard less than the one he has designed you to follow. You need a passionate desire to understand God's character before you can hope to understand his will. (One of my favorite books on God's character is *The Knowledge of the Holy* by A. W. Tozer—I highly encourage you to read it or another book that intimately explores the character of God.)

When you understand who God is, you come to the conclusion that not only is God's will *worth* submitting to, but you *must* submit to it.

FIGHTING OUR OWN WILL

But God's will isn't the only plan by which you could live your life—there are many plans you could potentially follow. You could follow the will of a friend or a parent. You could follow the will of an employer or of a spouse. But more often than not, there's one will that wars most violently against the "will of God"—your own.

The battle between your will and God's begins very early in your life, and it continues through the rest of it. At the crux of the battle are a feeling and a desire. The feeling is the strong persuasion that *you* know what's best for your life, and the desire is the strongest of human nature—to do what you *want* to do above everything else, even if it leads to your ultimate unhappiness or even destruction. The two are inextricably intertwined, and you war against these two every single day of your life. It's been that way since you were a little child, and will be that way until you die.

I have a front-row seat right now to observe the way in which the human will develops and this war rages in our lives: Andrea and I are in the first year of raising our first child. Our little boy is adorable. He's always wearing a smile, he's never met a stranger, and he laughs at everything. You can't imagine a cuter kid. The other day as we were giving him a bath, I got distracted, and as a result accidentally sprayed him in the face with water for a solid twenty seconds. If I were our little guy, I would have punched my dad. Instead our little boy took a deep breath, smiled from ear to ear, and let out a belly laugh. He's got a personality like few I've ever seen.

He's a wonderful kid, and yet he's already fighting this battle against his own will. It's been fascinating to watch. As he's moved from one phase of his development to the next—from rolling over to sitting up to crawling to walking—he has, without anyone else's input, decided to do what he wants, when he wants to do it. That's his will at work.

A few months ago this will was on full display and I was caught up in the battle. As a paranoid father, from the beginning I have paid very close attention to everything our doctor has told us about the common dangers associated with babies. I've read all the warning labels on every toy we've gotten him, and at any given moment you can find me staring at the baby monitor just making sure everything's okay. (Yes, I'm that type of father.) This hovering was never more evident than when Edward started rolling over. The doctor had told us that he should sleep on his back, not his stomach, but in the middle of the night, he would decide he wanted to sleep on his stomach and roll on over. So every time Edward would roll onto his stomach, I would walk into the room and carefully turn him onto his back.

It was comical. I would sneak in, creeping along the

floor, trying my hardest not to wake him. Then I would stand over the crib with my hands positioned in just the right way. I would grasp him and flip him in one fell swoop, and then I would tiptoe my way out of his room. Just about the time I got to the door, he would roll back onto his stomach. Then I would repeat the task, again and again. I did it what seemed like a thousand times, and without fail, Edward would immediately roll back onto his stomach. Our little boy had decided he was going to do what he wanted, not what I wanted him to do. That was his will at work.

It's human nature to obey your own will, to believe your own way is the best way, and to plan your life around your personal desires. This is rooted so deeply in our identity that we can't merely make a decision to change it. We literally have to change who we are, our very nature, in order to live differently.

What's most amazing about all of this is that most of us have a really bad track record when it comes to following our own personal advice. We know how easy it is to deceive ourselves, and we all have stories of how we've suffered for doing what we wanted to do over what we needed to do. Yet we keep trusting our own wills. Meanwhile, God's character isn't flawed like our own, nor is his track record so poor. He's entirely good, he's entirely trustworthy, and he's told us again and again that he is looking out for the best for our lives. Yet we keep trusting our flawed selves and ignoring the advice of the one who designed us and who is designing our lives.

It doesn't make a bit of sense—this constant fight over whether to follow our own will or God's. Maybe, just maybe, it's not necessary. Maybe we should just surrender.

THIS IS WHY

But what does all of this have to do with the confusion that surrounds the finding of God's will? It has everything to do with it. When our will is at war with God's, we are miserable; we second-guess ourselves, we are confused about what choices to make, and we fight to assert control over our own lives—control we were never meant to have, nor are equipped to handle. See, God doesn't make it easy to find the way because he knows it isn't easy for us to change this part of us—the part of us that will always pick what we want over what he wants.

So God makes this life a wrestling match, filled with ambiguity and confusion and unanswered questions and the kind of grueling heart-searching that you only experience when you're trying to answer questions whose consequences are profound. He allows this ambiguity so that we will fight our own will to trust his.

Pope Francis once spoke to a reporter about the reason for uncertainty in one's spiritual life:

[I]n this quest to seek and find God in all things there is still an area of uncertainty. There must be. If a person says that he met God with total certainty and is not touched by a margin of uncertainty, then this is not good. For me, this is an important key. If one has the answers to all the questions—that is the proof that God is not with him. It means that he is a false prophet using religion for himself. The great leaders of the people of God, like Moses, have always left room for doubt. You must leave room for the Lord, not for our certainties; we must be humble. Uncertainty is in every true discernment that is open to finding confirmation in spiritual consolation.[2]

If God just told us to do this or to do that, or if he made his plan for our life as clear as the words on this page, then we wouldn't fight as hard as we do against the part of us that wants to be in charge of the world. We struggle, precisely because we *do* want to know completely, but our desire for knowledge isn't an affront to God—it is a compliment to Him.

The apostle Paul faced the same struggle. He once wrote, "For now we see through a glass, darkly; but then face to face: now I know in part; but then shall I know even as also I am known" (1 Cor. 13:12 KJV). Paul knew that there would be seasons of uncertainty in one's spiritual life, and that those seasons were to be appreciated, not despised. The uncertainty doesn't mean that God has taken his hands off the steering wheel, but just that our own perspective is limited. We're on the highway of life and we have to trust that we are going in the right direction, even if we can't see the destination ahead. God does not design the world to trick us, to cripple us, to tease us by withholding from us the knowledge of his will, but God knows that we actually won't be helped by knowing whatever it is we are convinced would make our lives easier.

We want to know how he has ordained the rest of our lives—every detail and every decision. But guess what? He is never going to give us those answers. Because then we wouldn't need to walk in faith. We would either strut in arrogance, knowing the end goal of our lives and understanding the grandeur of the vision God intends us to carry out, or we would live in disappointment and bitterness because of the trials we will suffer and the obstacles we will face. If God told us everything, we wouldn't need God. So he doesn't, for our own good.

See, my friend Elliott will tell you that he never wanted to hear from God more than when he was trying to make a decision about changing his career. He never questioned himself more, never prayed more intensely, and had never before become so desperate to submit his will to God. Before that experience, his personal success made himself the center of the story. His professional trajectory was clear, he had job security, and he knew what was around the next bend. Then he received the job offer he didn't expect, and it forced him to get on his knees and to question his own confidence in himself. It was a battle between his will and God's will, and he was forced to dig deep and analyze his own heart. If God had made it easier, then he wouldn't have had to examine and clean up his heart so thoroughly.

It seems that our will and God's are diametrically opposed, continually at odds. When the will of man comes across the will of God, one of them has to die. But what if there was a way that our will and God's could actually be in total agreement? If our will could be something that would please God to have it carried out? Herein is the great secret of the will of God, and the answer to Satan's great lie: The will of God is more about *who* you are than where you are or what you do. You don't find it; you become it.

TWO

TERRORISTS MAKE GOOD PREACHERS

You are custom designed for your purpose

JOHN HAD THAT LOOK IN HIS EYE. THE I-DON'T-KNOW-what-I'm-supposed-to-do-with-my-life look, and he was making a beeline for me after church. As I've done many times before, I asked him to tell me about himself and what his dreams were, where he wanted to live and where he wanted to work. He told me he had a passion for business and always wanted to live in a big city. He really hoped to be successful one day so that he could help children in need around the world. He had gone on several missions trips to nations struggling with poverty, and he wanted to do something to help people struggling in that condition.

Within ten minutes I noticed that his weary eyes lit up when he started talking about certain things. He definitely had passions and dreams and there were things he wanted to do with his life. He just didn't realize it.

"So what do you think?" he asked. "What does God want me to do with my life? What is God's will for my life?"

I told him that God probably wanted him to be a businessman in a big city and that God wanted him to be successful and generous and that he ought to start working on that immediately. He wasn't convinced.

"But how do I know that's what God wants me to do with my life?" he said.

"Because he made you for it," was my reply.

He thought God might want him to be a missionary because of how deeply he was affected when he traveled overseas, and he really, really loved the Lord, so he thought maybe God might be calling him into full-time ministry. It didn't occur to him that God might have actually designed him in a particular way for a job that only he could do, and that God's will for him might be exactly what he wanted to do with his life because that's how he was made. He hadn't yet learned that God's will is more about *who* you are than *where* you are. God's will was—for John—hidden in plain sight.

EXHIBIT A—THE APOSTLE PAUL

It's popular within "Christian speak" to refer to the apostle Paul as the "least likely person to change the world." After all, you would never expect a former terrorist, walking to Damascus with letters in hand authorizing the murder of Christians, to be converted and become the person God would use to spread the gospel from one end of the Roman Empire to the other.

Preachers teach that Paul was not the type of person you or I would have assigned such a great responsibility. He was "the least likely" person for God to use in this profound and powerful way. He didn't fit the bill. But that isn't true at all. When you take a closer look at Paul's pedigree, you discover that even this "terrorist" was custom designed by God for the passion that God would eventually put on his heart. Even before Saul-the-terrorist became Paul-the-preacher, God had scripted his life to prepare him for his ultimate purpose.

First, Paul had a zealous personality and was deeply religious. It's clear that when he committed to do something, he committed to it with all of his might. That's why he wasn't just opposing Christianity; he was trying to destroy it. Paul had this all-or-nothing attitude with everything. Even as a kid he was probably the type of child who would play a pick-up basketball game with the intensity of a world championship. He didn't do anything halfheartedly. If he was going to oppose Christianity, he was going to try and wipe it off the planet. And when he became its greatest church planter, he was going to do it in every major city along every major road.

Paul took his zeal with him into his faith, and it would allow him to persevere in the most demanding and dangerous situations. He would preach the gospel in the most hazardous places, and press on when he had to endure everything from a shipwreck and snakebite to multiple imprisonments, beatings, and trials. Paul was zealous. It was at the heart of who he was. That was who God made him to be, and when that personality was submitted under *God's will*, not *Paul's will*, it became the force upon which Christianity grew from an insignificant sect into a global religion in one generation.

Second, Paul was highly educated and well acquainted with the culture of his time. He grew up in a city called Tarsus in the province of Silicia. Tarsus was the most important city in Silicia. Cicero once lived there, it was where Antony and Cleopatra met, and Julius Caesar had even visited the city. A famous Roman geographer "described the people of Tarsus as avidly pursuant of culture, the study of philosophy, the liberal arts, and 'the whole round of learning in general'—so much so that Tarsus in this respect at least surpassed even Athens and Alexandria. . . . Tarsus, in short, was what we might call 'a university city.'"[1]

Third, Paul was a deeply committed Jew. Philippians 3:5 says that Paul was a "Hebrew of Hebrews" (NIV). It describes him as a member of the tribe of Benjamin, and his faithfulness to Judaism is even indicated by the fact that his parents originally named him Saul after a famous Benjamite. Paul spoke of his commitment to Judaism in Galatians 1:14, "I was advancing in Judaism beyond many of my own age among my people and was extremely zealous for the traditions of my fathers" (NIV). And indeed he was, because we know that Paul also studied in Jerusalem under the most famous Jewish teacher of Paul's time, Gamaliel. Some people speculate that Paul's zeal was even evident in his relationship with Gamaliel, based upon a Jewish text where Gamaliel describes one of his students as always trying to refute him.[2]

Finally, Paul was a Roman citizen. This saved his life in Jerusalem when an uprising among the Jewish leaders threatened his demise, and later it allowed him to appeal his conviction to Caesar, eventually leading to the conversion of members of Caesar's own household in Rome and probably an opportunity for Paul to share the story of Jesus Christ with Caesar himself! It would have been extraordinarily unusual for a Jewish family in Tarsus to have Roman citizenship. No one really knows how Paul's family received this honor, which wasn't often conferred among those living outside of Rome, but he had this citizenship and it opened enormous doors for him during his ministry. One scholar even speculates that Paul's family, a family probably known for making tents, had provided tents to Roman soldiers and was rewarded with citizenship as a result. We don't know how the family received this honor, and we probably won't ever know, but having it provided plenty of opportunities for Paul as he traveled around the Roman Empire preaching the gospel.

So, to recap, Paul was a zealous man, trained in Judaism, educated in a highly cultured city, and he had the elite status of a Roman citizen. He was probably also from a wealthy and influential family given the education he had received and the travel he had embarked on to receive it.

All things considered, he was perfectly fit to be a missionary to the Roman Empire. See, if you want to understand the world in which Christ lived, and in which Paul preached, you need only to understand three things: Roman government, Jewish religion, and Greek culture.[3] Those are the three keys to understanding the world of Paul and Christ. At the time, Rome ruled the world, the Jewish religion was at the heart of the region where Christianity grew up and was also spread in pockets around the entire empire, and Greek culture (called "Hellenism") had been spread by Alexander the Great across that entire part of the world to the degree that nearly everyone spoke Greek, loved Greek culture, and understood Greek philosophy.

Paul wasn't the least likely kind of person to be able to

interact so competently with so many people in the Roman Empire—he was the *most* likely person. His unlikelihood only went as far as his need for conversion from radical Judaism to Christianity, but once he converted, he was custom made to slide into the role that God had destined him to fill. He wasn't trying to find God's will for his life— Paul was just being who he was created to be and God's will caught up with him. And although his future was certainly not what Saul would have anticipated, the characteristics that would make him a great missionary were there long before he walked down that road to Damascus.

And Paul isn't the only one. History is filled with the stories of those whom God had prepared for a plan long before they realized it. Billy Graham was once asked this question: "What will be your first question to God when you reach heaven?"

He answered, "I have often said the first thing I am going to do when I get to heaven is to ask, 'Why me, Lord? Why did you choose a farm boy from North Carolina to preach to so many people?'"[4]

Yet who better to preach to the masses in America in his time period of history than someone so well acquainted with the life of the masses? Billy didn't grow up with a silver spoon in his mouth. He grew up experiencing the same kind of life that most Americans experienced during his time in history. He was a "regular" person whom God has used to reach 215 million "regular" people in 185 countries.

And it's not just religious figures who are custom designed for their purpose. Sometimes we don't even know how fitted we are for the plan God has in mind for us. Take Sergeant York, for example. Alvin York was born in a one-room log cabin in Pall Mall, Tennessee, on December 13, 1887, into a family of eleven children. He grew up hunting with his father and being taught Scripture by his parents. They were extremely poor Alvin's entire life, and when his father died when Alvin was just twenty-four, he became the primary breadwinner for his family. The frustrations of his job as a laborer led him into drinking, fighting, and gambling in order to vent his frustration. But this life of debauchery eventually gave way when he was radically touched by the grace of God.

Despite his formerly violent past, York's conversion made him a pacifist, and he was deeply troubled when the notice came ordering him to register to be drafted. He believed that it was against the will of God for him to fight, and he attempted to file four times for conscientious objector status. He was denied each time. Within three weeks of the last denial, he was drafted into the army. But God had a different plan. York's division was assigned to rescue another division that had been trapped behind enemy lines. Their objective was to scale the hill at Chatel-Chéhéry, which was heavily guarded by German machine guns, and rescue the lost division from where they lay trapped behind the lines. And there York discovered that he was exactly prepared for his job.

Sneaking up the side of the hill, they found twenty or so unarmed Germans having breakfast. They captured the Germans just as machine-gun fire burst out over the clearing. Nine Americans fell dead or wounded. York dropped to the ground and began firing at the operators of the machine guns. Years of hunting turkeys with his father suddenly became invaluable; he shot off round after round at the enemy. Eventually the Germans surrendered. When counted, the prisoners numbered more than one hundred and thirty. York had killed thirty-six Germans on his own, including several officers.

York was promoted to sergeant for his bravery, and was decorated with seven medals from four countries, including the Congressional Medal of Honor and the French Croix de Guerre. This one-time farm boy from Tennessee became one of the most decorated soldiers of World War I. All of his life experiences, which started in that one-room log cabin, prepared him for what became his destiny.[5]

In our limited and finite minds, God's will may not make sense, but God is always at work preparing us. We are born in the family we are born into for a reason, raised with the experiences we've had for a reason, and not one event in our lives is ever wasted. Though we may be surprised by the plan God has for us, the talents, personality traits, and experiences necessary for us to play our part in it are formed in us long before we understand why we have them.

This should give us great faith that we are custom designed for God's plan. He made us with great care for our individual mission.

GOD MADE YOU

The single most defining characteristic about God's relationship with man is that God is man's maker. God designed us, and he custom designed us. He didn't make a world of robots with the same components. He made a world where individuals speak and look different and are even different colors. He made a world where every single living human being would have his or her own unique fingerprint and DNA. God loves diversity, and he took great care to make a world that celebrated it in its most fantastic form.

He didn't make you to become like anyone else.

He made you to be you, and he designed you as you are for a reason. He created you to fill a particular place in his will, like a puzzle piece that fits into the one and only place to complete the picture. If you want to know what it is that God wants you to do, then first ask yourself, "Who am I really?" Analyze your family and your unique life experiences. Look at what makes you happy and what you enjoy the most. Pay attention to what you dream about and how you wish the world worked. In all of this, you'll find what makes you unique, and you'll also find what it is that God designed you to do with your life. He didn't design you to be anyone else, to have anyone else's gifts, or to do anyone else's mission. He designed you to make your own unique contribution to the world, and it gives him glory when you decide to be who he made you to be and to do what he designed you to do.

Erik Rees takes it one step further by providing a five-word acrostic—SHAPE—for us to use to discover how God has "shaped us for service": spiritual gifts, heart, abilities, personality, and experiences.[6] We all have God-given "spiritual gifts" (like evangelism or giving), we all have passions (things we love to do) that are our "heart," we have "abilities," which are our natural inclinations, we have unique "personalities" (some of us like routine, for instance, and others like variety), and we have had experiences in our vocations, with our families, and through our educations or painful seasons. Erik believes these shape "who we are" and guide us to our place of service. I agree with him.

JUST BE YOU

One of the interesting problems of the early church involved regular people wanting to leave their occupations to serve the church in the way that Paul did. People were powerfully converted and deeply touched by the gospel, and they thought that the next logical step would be to enter into "full-time" ministry.

Individuals who were working regular jobs in the community became so passionate about the gospel that they were tempted to leave their lives behind and become missionaries like Paul. They didn't think their "secular" lives and jobs were as important as "sacred" ones like the job Paul was doing. While there was certainly a place for this, Paul discouraged most people from doing it. He did not believe that most people should serve Christ in the way he did, but that the gospel would be better served if they stayed in their jobs, continued living in their communities, and put their conversion on display within the context in which they lived and worked.

In 1 Corinthians 7:20 he wrote, "Each man must remain in that condition in which he was called" (NASB). Before that, in verse 17, he said, "Only, as the Lord has assigned to each one, as God has called each, in this manner let him walk" (NASB).

Paul was saying, "God has assigned you to the place where *you* are. It is God that made you and he wants to use you as you are, where you are." This became the secret to the explosive growth of Christianity in the first and second centuries. It grew from one end of the empire to the other because Christians were literally imbedded in culture, everywhere. They worked the same jobs, shopped in the same places, participated in the same hobbies, and lived their changed lives on display among those whom they had always known.

God had made them as he did, and put them where they were, because he had a plan for their lives just as he had for Paul. When Paul was arguing with the philosophers in Athens or the rabbis in Jerusalem, arguing his case in front of Caesar, or continuing on to one more city when everyone else had given up, I think Paul would have said he felt as if he was "made for this." And that is the first sign that you're on the path to God's plan for your life, submitted under his will—it's when you feel like saying, "I was made for this." It's not your location, or even your vocation. It's not whether you're in full-time ministry or working on Wall Street. That's because the will of God is about *who* you are, and it starts *where* you already are.

THREE

CEILING FANS AND LITTLE WHITE DOGS

Should I wait on God?

HAVE YOU EVER ASKED GOD FOR A SIGN? MY FRIEND Johnny did it once. He was walking down a street in the downtown area of the small Virginia town where I used to live when he prayed, "Dear God, if a little white dog walks around the corner of that building, then I will know that you want me to ask Sarah out." Then he stood there for a half hour, watching in anticipation, wondering if God was going to answer his prayer. He almost gave up a half dozen times, but he just couldn't let himself walk away lest he miss God's answer to his desperate prayer.

Just when he was about to leave in dismay, because he really wanted to ask Sarah out, he heard the distant bark of a small dog. His eyes bulged out of his head, and he listened more closely and looked intently at the corner of that building just as a small *black* dog walked around the corner.

It threw him for an absolute loop. Maybe he had prayed for a black dog, not a white one, or maybe he hadn't mentioned the color of the dog whatsoever in his prayer, or maybe God was telling him that he ought to date Sarah's equally attractive roommate who was wearing black the last time he saw her? Or maybe God was telling him that dating Sarah was a bad idea because her heart wasn't pure and white, but dark like sin? Or maybe the dog was actually white but had rolled around in some ashes or tar or something? He was totally confused.

The whole thing seems nuts, right? But how often have you and I asked God for a sign and been just as frantic in our interpretation?

THE WISDOM OF CEILING FANS

Actually, we have devised all kinds of crazy methods to figure out God's will or to ask God to figure it out for us. I once heard about a guy who turned on the ceiling fan in his apartment and opened up his Bible on his bed so the breeze coming from the fan could flip through the pages. He waited till the pages stopped flipping, and then he looked with anticipation to discover the verses that were "revealed to him by God." Well, it turns out that God really likes to reveal verses about divine judgment when one tries to use a ceiling fan to determine his plan!

Others read the story of Gideon in Judges 6 and decide to put out "their own fleece"—literally, praying for God to send them an undeniable sign to help with their decision about what major to choose or job to take. Others climb mountains and wait for God to speak to them in an audible voice, listening for some little whispery noise to float to them on the wind. Lots of Christians expect lightning bolts from heaven or writing on the wall. They bargain with God in hopes that he will show them his will. I've done it all myself, and my favorite—and most embarrassing—incidents have involved my asking God for a sign in such detail that I couldn't remember what exactly I had asked him to do for me!

Jesus had something to say about all of this, and it wasn't the most politically correct statement he made: "An evil and adulterous generation seeks for a sign, but no sign will be given" (Matt. 16:4 ESV).

Could that be any clearer?

God doesn't want us testing him in this type of way.

Period.

Often all of this testing, all of this back and forth, is more about us than it is about God. It is a desperate attempt to weasel our way out of faith and the responsibility of making our own decisions. Then we spiritualize the entire process by saying that we are "relying on the Lord" or "waiting on God's will." In turn, we feel good about ourselves for "relying on God" when in actuality we're desperately attempting to absolve ourselves of any personal responsibility.

Yet at the heart of Christian theology is the idea that God has given man free will. He gives us the ability to make choices and the information we need to make good ones. When we relinquish that ability and push the choice back to God, we are virtually giving up that freedom, telling him that we do not appreciate this gift he has given us. This is neither honoring to God nor beneficial to us. Our free will is what makes us human. It's what allows us the ability to love and to make choices and to become who it is that we want to be. It is a gift from God, and it is an insult to God when we choose to ignore it.

WAITING ON GOD . . . OR IS GOD WAITING ON US?

Young evangelicals are constantly told that our teen, college, and young adult years are a "waiting period." We're waiting for jobs, for spouses, for God's calling. This isn't the season to get to work, but the season to wait until God shows us what we're supposed to do with our lives. So we're supposed to pray and to wait for an answer, and when the answers don't come, that's when we start asking God to "send a yellow pigeon into our bedroom window at five p.m. on Thursday" if he wants us to be a missionary to a tribe of pigmy people. Since the end to the waiting period is vague, we start getting increasingly desperate to know what's next, and then the prayers get crazier and crazier.

This kind of "spiritual waiting" isn't helpful; it's actually harmful. We may think it is grounded in faith, but it often comes out of fear. We are so afraid that we'll do something God doesn't want us to do that we demand proof after proof of his will so that we can make faithless, risk-free decisions. We are so afraid of taking a chance on what we might think is God's will that we try to shift responsibility entirely to him, asking for him to give us a miracle and then while we're waiting for the miracle we tell our friends that we are "waiting on God." We want him to remove from the decision all of the ambiguity and uncertainty. That way, if things go wrong, we can shake our heads and tell ourselves that "everything happens for a reason," and comfort ourselves with the thought that at least we did what God told us to do.

But did we?

Is this how God speaks to us?

This idea of "waiting for God to move" lulls us into the belief that these years—some of the most important years of our lives—when our habits and personalities are being formed, when we learn how to function in relationships and in the workplace, are not really that important after all. It shifts responsibility from us to God, leaving us free to waste our time with video games, fool around with relationships without serious intentions, and distract ourselves from our future plans with the technology and its drama we invite upon ourselves. This is one of the reasons why "thirty is the new twenty," why our generation struggles to focus on serious things, and why we so egregiously delay adulthood. We agonize over decisions and often put them off, saying that we are waiting for confirmation from God that we are doing the right thing. In the meantime, we fill the space between "asking" and "hearing" by wasting valuable time on meaningless pursuits. Rather than swimming ahead, we're just treading water, looking for a blinking sign to drop from the sky and tell us where to go and what to do.

We want God to answer all the "W" questions for us first—the who, what, when, and where. But is this really necessary? I don't think it is. I don't think we should embrace this type of attitude; instead we ought to embrace an attitude that believes that *now* is as important as the future, and that so much of the will of God is realized in the everyday decisions and moments that we can let roll by unrecognized while we're waiting for God to answer bigger questions and to provide us with supernatural signs. Meanwhile, every season of life is equally important and every daily encounter matters just as much as future goals, and somehow these passing moments, which you're tempted to discount, are actually the building blocks for your future.

Whether right or wrong, my personal story runs contrary to this "waiting game." I started my career at Liberty University, at the invitation of our founder, before I was twenty years old. I was thrown into the deep end without the knowledge or experience necessary for the responsibility I was given, but our university's founder believed in on-the-job training and believed young leaders could do just that—lead. And I'm so glad he did. Now I've just entered my thirties, but I have more than a decade of experience in higher education. I've had a lifetime of opportunities and challenges while still so young, and I just can't imagine what it would be like if I was only getting my start now!

Yet nearly every twentysomething I know is playing this waiting game; rather than jumping in with both feet, they are twiddling their thumbs, waiting for a dove to descend from the sky or a dog to walk around the corner of a building. Meanwhile God has them—us—in lives that keep on ticking, day after day, and he's given us a book filled with words of advice that we're to apply to our lives every single day. There is always a logical direction to follow, a next nearest step to take, and often the will of God is more about following that next nearest step than it is about waiting for God to send a sign. It's about being the person God would have you be in whatever situation he has you at the moment.

Sometimes we say that we're "waiting on God" when God is actually waiting on us. He is expecting us to start taking life seriously and start taking advantage of the opportunities he has already given us, as opposed to waiting for the next new thing. He's expecting us to live our current season to its fullest.

THE STORY OF KATIE DAVIS

When I think about people who stopped waiting for later and started working on God's will, I'm inspired by the story of Katie Davis. This high school student knew that God intended her to do something out of the ordinary, something she would never have planned on her own, and something that was beyond herself.

She was only sixteen when she told her parents about this feeling, and they responded by sending her on a three-week missions trip to Uganda. While there, she fell in love with the country, with the people, and most of all with the children in the orphanage where she served. This former homecoming queen, class president, top-of-her-class student was so moved that she convinced her parents to let her postpone college for a year and spend that time in Uganda, living and working in the orphanage. She lived in a room that was only three by six feet, and spent her days ministering to the orphanage's 102 children. She changed diapers, fed babies, played with the older children, and realized that a year would not be enough to do all she wanted to in this poverty-stricken country.

So she did something radical, something that no doubt caused her many a sleepless night before the decision was made. She picked up her entire life—leaving behind her friends, her schooling, her family—and moved to Uganda permanently at the age of nineteen. She didn't put it off, waiting for a sign from God. She didn't wait until a convenient season of her life came around or even until everyone around her supported her decision.

She just went.

Katie is twenty-two now. She is the adopted mother to fourteen children, eleven of whom are homeschooled. She spends her days taking care of them and anyone else who comes her way seeking help. She gives food to the hungry, medical care to the sick, and love to every person she comes into contact with. Why? Because she didn't wait for writing on the wall.

In her amazing book *Kisses from Katie*, she wrote: "I don't always know where this life is going. I can't see the end of the road, but here is the great part: Courage is not about knowing the path. It is about taking the first step. It is about Peter getting out of the boat, stepping out onto the water with complete faith that Jesus will not let him drown."[1]

And while Katie's story is certainly unusual and not a model for most, it does provide inspiration for all of us to stop idling on life's highway. It's time to put our feet on the pedal and *go*. Katie took her step of faith, a step that took her across the globe and into a life that she never imagined. She understands that she is exactly where she needs to be, doing exactly what she was designed to do. It all started with that first step; the end of waiting for God to move her and the beginning of moving herself forward into his will for her life. As Katie wrote, "It may take place in a foreign land or it may take place in your backyard, but I believe that we were each created to change the world for *someone*. To serve *someone*. To love *someone* the way Christ first loved us, to spread His light. This is the dream, and it is possible."[2]

God's will isn't something you find to live later. It's something that's beginning now. The only sign that God's given you is the fact that you have breath to breathe. Now that's a real miracle.

FOUR

ALEXANDER THE WHAT?

Get moving, till God stops you

PAUL WAS THE FIRST MISSIONARY, AND HE WAS A FAN-
tastic one. He took seriously Jesus' closing words to all
of his followers to "be his witnesses" (see Acts 1:8), and
so Paul set out to preach the gospel to the ends of the
empire. He made tents along the way, earning his own
keep, and he planted churches so thoroughly that he finished his work from Jerusalem to what is now northern
Italy.[1]

But why did Paul go where he went and when he did?
Maybe Paul went through a grueling time of decision. He
may have prayed until his knees were raw and fasted till
his cheeks became cavernous. Paul probably spent weeks,

even months, wrestling with the question of where God wanted him to take the gospel and in what way he wanted him to preach it. Maybe Paul himself pleaded with God to answer that awful question, "What am I supposed to do with my life?"

Because this is how *we* make big, important life decisions, right? We enter into an exhausting season filled with penitent prayers and second-guessing ourselves. Eventually we often just give up and do something—anything—all the while unsure if we've done the right thing.

But there is no indication that Paul did any of this wrestling. The church commissioned Paul and Barnabas to go preach the gospel abroad, as the first missionaries, and they just did it. They went preaching in cities along the primary roadways. Paul even preached in prisons when he was incarcerated. Along the way he discovered enormous opportunities to share Christ with rich and poor alike. The story reads like a great epic filled with shipwrecks and riots, miracles and demon possession, and even moments where Paul was afforded fantastic opportunities to speak with the most influential political leaders of his time while the masses watched and heard.

"But," you might ask, "*why* did Paul go to the places where he went, preach to the people he did, and plant the churches he planted?" It's simple—Paul went to the cities he went to because they were large and influential. Paul preached in the synagogues he preached in because, as a Jew who was trained by a top Jewish scholar, he could. Paul went to spend time with the philosophers in Athens because Paul grew up entrenched in the Greek culture that held together the Roman Empire. As I've already said, the key to understanding the New Testament is Roman politics, Jewish religion, and Greek culture. Paul was a master of each.

Clearly he was custom designed for these missionary journeys.

When he wrote, "I have become all things to all people so that by all possible means I might save some" (1 Cor. 9:22 NIV), he wasn't talking about becoming someone he wasn't. He was talking about his ability to adapt to different situations and different environments because of his personality, his education, and his life experience. The issue wasn't knowing what to do, but knowing who he was. It reminds me of what Richard Stearns, the president of World Vision, has written in his book *Unfinished*: "God created you intentionally to play a very specific role in his unfolding story. God didn't create any extras meant to just stand on the sidelines and watch the story unfold; he created players meant to be on center stage. And you will feel fully complete only when you discover the role you were born to play."[2]

Paul was fulfilling his role. He didn't "pray about it." He just did what made sense. Take, for example, Paul's account in 1 Thessalonians 3:1. He stated, "We thought it best" (NIV) before he went on to explain a decision to travel to a particular place. There is no mention of prayer, just Paul justifying his decision and then moving on to the next city. He just went, and went about praying as he went. It was entirely logical that Paul would preach in big cities (where there were more people), and that Paul would preach in synagogues (where Christianity's Jewish roots found good soil). It made sense that Paul would preach to Romans and Jews (because he was both), and that he would take full advantage of the culture of his time when he was developing his sermon illustrations and making his arguments.

In hindsight, if you know anything about the Roman Empire, Paul's story looks awfully logical, maybe even expected. Paul was just doing what made sense for him, and it worked like a charm in the world he was living in. It was God who was making something out of it all, but it was Paul who was deciding where to go and what to do.

BUT HOW IS GOD INVOLVED?

When I start teaching this way, the immediate criticism I receive is that my mentality about God's will is too human-centric. People say, "Surely you're not encouraging people not to pray about what they're going to do with their life, where they're going to live, what job they are going to take, who they are going to marry?" Of course I am not encouraging people to forsake praying over these consequential parts of life. I'm simply saying that you ought to pray as you go, and that the Bible clearly teaches us that if there's no clear direction, then God is giving you the freedom to use the good brain he's given you to make a choice between options, all of which might be just fine. That's part of the adventure—and not the problem—of life. But more on that later.

The second common criticism I hear is that this way of thinking about God's will discounts the hand of God in man's life and work. They say, "You're robbing God of the glory he deserves for the work that he did in Paul's life, or anyone's life for that matter." But that's not the case either. It's just that God works in an even more profound and remarkable way than we've ever imagined. The common idea we have is that we ought to pray each decision to death and wait until God gives us a blinking light in the sky, but that doesn't give God the glory he deserves either. It paints the picture of a last-minute and indecisive God who is a little too busy with other things to answer our prayers.

As I've said already, I truly believe that wrestling to find God's will is a process of spiritual development that forces us to suppress our will and submit to God's will for us. It's less about the answer than about what desiring the answer does to our own sense of self-importance and self-assurance.

As for God's glory, it is most clearly seen in the big picture. It's seen more clearly from thirty thousand feet up than from standing with two feet on the ground. And when you see God's will in this way, it really does look remarkable. He's not just involved in your life; he's building the world around it. He's been moving the chess pieces for centuries with you in mind.

In the case of Paul, God's glory is seen in the way God prepared the world for Paul's message, and—get this—he had been preparing it for centuries. Historians have made the point that the Roman Empire itself was custom designed for the explosion of Christianity, and they're right. It all began in the fourth century BC (more than three hundred years before Christ) when Alexander the Great began conquering the world. He brought with him the Greek language and Greek culture and, for the first time in history, a common language and a common culture united a wide swath of land.[3] This meant that a missionary like Paul could preach over hundreds of miles of territory in one language. He wouldn't have to learn the languages of the individual cities and regions because nearly everyone spoke Greek; even many Jews in their synagogues spoke Greek, for their Old Testament had been translated into the language. While Alexander the Great was conquering the world, God was unveiling the first part of his plan to conquer Satan. Alexander *the Great* was God's pawn, his chess piece that he was using to prepare the world for his Son's triumphant entry. Alexander was, unbeknownst to him, doing God's bidding.

In addition, the Roman Empire presided over the construction of common roadways that went from one end of the empire to the other. These main roads connected all the metropolitan areas, and because everyone used the same roads, they were more secure than traditional methods of travel. Rome built these roads to facilitate commerce and fuel their economy, and also so that their armies could easily get from place to place in order to secure the empire and pat down any rebellion. Rome thought they were building roads to protect the sovereignty of their empire, but it was actually God's hand carving those freeways out of rock and desert so that his Son's life message would have free course through all of Rome. In fact, every road had an *intinerarium*, like an ancient road map that listed the towns and settlements you could reach if you used that particular road. It even cited the distance to each. The Roman Empire, for the first time in history, allowed travelers to plan where they were going and how long it would take to get them there, making it easy for Paul to travel extensively throughout the region.

Finally, during the time of Jesus and Paul, the Roman Empire was enjoying what scholars have referred to as the "Pax Romana." It was a two-hundred-year period of relative peace and minimal expansion during which the Roman Empire flourished in almost every way. This mattered immensely to the growth of Christianity because it brought a unified rule to the Mediterranean world—and with it an end to the almost constant warfare there since the death of Alexander the Great. Even on the frontiers of the empire there were extended periods of peace. The blessings of a single, stable government were an important factor in the growth and spread of Christianity.

Because of all of this happening in the Roman Empire, the gospel was able to move quickly, efficiently, and peacefully during the time of the apostle Paul. God had been working his will for centuries, preparing the world, preparing Paul, and preparing the hearts of millions for the arrival of the gospel.

GO TILL GOD STOPS YOU

Paul traveled the Roman roads to the places where the people were, and when he finished in one big city he just went along to the next one. He went as he was, utilizing his gifts and fueled by his passions, walking through the doors that seemed open to him and leaving behind those doors that were clearly closed. Paul didn't leave his vocation behind, but took his tent-making business with him, and worked hard so that he wouldn't have to rely upon the support of others. No doubt his tent making also provided a wonderful opportunity for him to meet plenty of people in the cities he visited.

Paul didn't pray till God told him where to go and then stay there until God told him where to go next. He sort of went with the flow. He stayed long enough to accomplish his goals, but not so long that he would wear out his welcome or make the church too reliant upon his leadership. Logic was Paul's friend, not his enemy, and again, he just did what made sense. He didn't wait until God showed him where to go; he just went until God stopped him, and that's the missing key to so many people's understanding of God's will. God's will is more about going till he stops you than waiting until he starts you.

In three missionary journeys, covering a large portion of the Roman Empire, God only intervened in this way on two significant occasions. On one occasion Paul had a vision of a man from Macedonia pleading with him to come preach to them, and on another occasion Paul was heading to Asia when the "spirit of Christ" kept him from going (Acts 6). In either case, there was no ambiguity as to whether God was speaking to him. There was no second-guessing—it was crystal clear—and I think the same thing will be true of us in the rare circumstance when God shows up in order to stop us. It will be so clear that we won't dare question whether or not it was him.

Just as he did with Paul, God intervenes when necessary in our lives in order to ensure that his will is accomplished. This means that we don't have to be terrified about the consequences of our choices; God is never surprised by our choices, never horrified, even when we think we've ruined our lives with a bad decision. He takes this into account as he organizes the world and writes our own stories. You can rest assured that our benevolent God will intervene if we get off course. Sometimes we'll find him quietly, invisibly moving the world on our behalf, and occasionally we might find a door slammed in our faces to keep us from going the wrong way. Regardless, it's his job to keep us on track, and our job to just do our best. He knows us, and is comfortable with our imperfections. He knew what he was getting himself into when he brought us into his family.

This ought to be a source of constant comfort for us when we are fighting to decide how we want to move forward in our lives, and when we bite our lips and take the next logical step. Actually, it takes more faith to do this than it does to follow a pillar of fire in the right direction. Faith is only necessary when we don't know exactly where we're going, and we have to hold on to belief that God is walking by our side.

In other words, it's our job to keep our car on the road. He'll take care of the guardrails, and he's got quite the track record. No one has ever driven off his road.

FIVE

FORKS IN THE ROAD

How to decide when both paths look good

EMILY HAD THREE JOB OFFERS SITTING ON HER DESK. She was lucky to have anything at all in the economy she was living in, and now she had not one opportunity, but three. She knew she should feel blessed to be in such a wonderful situation, but she just wished she only had one option. That would have made the decision simpler, but now she was facing a huge dilemma that would affect the next phase of her life—maybe the rest of her life. And she had no idea how to decide.

What would I tell Emily? I would tell her to think clearly about each. Look at how each might contribute to her spiritual, financial, emotional, physical, vocational, and relational well-being and then just pick one. Simple enough, right? But the act of choosing when the choice may affect the rest of your life becomes anything but simple. We fear making a mistake, making a "bad" decision, as if one of the options God has presented to us is actually a trick and some kind of metaphysical buzzer will go off if we pick that one.

God doesn't do trick questions.

The options before you may really and truly be equal, and you really and truly have the power to choose. You also don't have to worry about making the wrong decision and thus flicking a domino that will relegate the rest of your life to a consecutive series of other failures. Emily should just make a decision, and then make it a good decision by how she handles it.

If it all looks the same on paper, then you're free to decide based on any basis you like (maybe one city is cooler than the others or one has a better mall or is near the beach or the mountains). Just decide. You can even put the names of each job in a hat and draw one, and unless God drops a brick out of the sky on your head, you'll be making a good decision.

Why?

Because God gives us free will; not to make his will subject to ours, but to give us the joy of navigating through life like an adventure, so that we might know the joy of choosing good things. We have the chance to choose a goal and set out after it without being afraid that the path we choose is the wrong one.

God's will cannot be destroyed by any choice we make. It is not so fragile that one misstep on our part will shatter it. It is stronger than our mistakes; in fact, it can even *use* our mistakes to further its ends. Our mistakes are not wasted, thrown into the metaphysical garbage pail. They become our lessons, the foundation of our future choices. They become the ways we relate to others, because God in his wisdom even allows different people to go through the same struggles so that we can help those who come after us. As a popular worship song says, "nothing is wasted." So we can make our choices without fear. We can move forward knowing that nothing we do can take us outside of God's will.

CHOICES, CHOICES, CHOICES

The Bible is absolutely full of people making choices. God gives the Israelites choices to make about what they would believe or how they would participate in his plan to get them to the promised land. As a result, they make good decisions and they make bad ones. In Deuteronomy 1, for instance, they decide not to trust God as he is leading them into the promised land, and as a result that entire generation died wandering around the desert waiting for another generation to rise up with the faith to follow God's will over their own. In Deuteronomy 2 and 3 they begin to make better choices and are rewarded for it by the possession of parts of the land that God had promised them. Before that, God gave Moses the choice whether he would stand up to Pharaoh or stay a vagabond in the desert (Exodus 3–4), and before that, God gave Abraham a choice as to whether he would be willing to sacrifice his son Isaac (Genesis 22).

Actually, you could read the entire Bible from cover to cover and discover in nearly every story a moment of consequential decision. In God's sovereign plan, he's often leading us to points of decision, and we often have an expectation of divine intervention in the most important decisions in our lives. But, more often than not, God chooses not to intervene. He forces us to decide.

This is actually part of what makes the Christian concept of God so unique, especially when compared to the common, pagan ideas of God in the first century. As Christians, we believe that every human being is made in the image of God. This theology dignifies humanity. While we are subject to God, we also have the image of God inside of us, and having that glimpse of God in us is a way that God honors us as human beings. God took great pride, at least in a small way, in making us like himself.

The prevailing pagan idea of the relationship between

man and god in the first century didn't contain this dig-
nifying idea. Man was chiefly considered subject to the
gods, and man didn't have the ability to assert himself in
any form. He had no dignity, no rights, and no personal
communication with the gods. His will was always forci-
bly subject to the gods' will, but in Christianity we believe
that the very fact that we have a will is representative of
the image of God in us.

God has given us the gift of freedom to make our
own decisions, and when we reject that freedom, it is an
insult to the Creator who gave us this incredible privi-
lege. It honors God for us to invite him into our decision
making by seeking the wisdom of Scripture or praying
about different components of those decisions, but too
often we're not going to God for advice, but with the
expectation that he will decide for us. When we do this,
it's not only lazy, it's a dishonor to the one who carefully
designed you so that you would have everything you
need for life (2 Peter 1:3). It is not only God's expectation
that we would use what he's given us to make decisions
about life, but it is a way of giving him glory.

It's like when a mentor watches his protégé do
something well. That makes the mentor proud that
his investment was treated responsibly, and he is honored when he watches the one he taught apply what he
has learned. On the contrary, if that mentor's protégé
ignored all he had been taught and insisted on asking the

mentor to do it for him, then that would be dishonoring. The same is true of God and man. God has given us the capacity to choose. He has given us the gift of being able to make our own choices, and when we refuse we are disregarding that gift.

HOW TO CHOOSE

God is especially honored when we consult his guidebook—the Bible—for the wisdom we need to make those decisions. The Bible is filled with practical advice for everyday life and with stories of people who were struggling through almost every emotion, challenge, or situation imagineable. The Bible has a lot to say about a lot of things, but you know, as I do, that it doesn't cover everything you could face in your life.

It's like a student, Ethan, once said to me, "I know the Bible tells me I shouldn't sleep around or murder someone, but the Bible isn't going to help me decide whether to live in California or South Carolina or to work for Boeing or Lockheed Martin. So when you tell me to look into God's Word for wisdom, I'm kind of stuck."

I gave Ethan two verses that I believe are the most important verses in the Bible when it comes to these types of decisions—and by "decisions" I mean the ambiguous ones, whether you are deciding on where you're going to live or how you will plan your future. These two verses are your guides. The first deals mainly with amoral decisions and the second with moral considerations, but they each can also apply to either. I believe you should write these verses down or plug them into your smartphone and carry them with you everywhere you go. They can be your guide through many of life's greatest and most difficult decisions.

Here they are:

The heart of man plans his way,
> but the LORD establishes his steps. (Prov. 16:9 ESV)

All things are lawful for me, but all things are not helpful. (1 Cor. 6:12 NKJV)

From a moralistic perspective, Paul said in 1 Corinthians 6:12 that just because something is not wrong to do doesn't mean that it's the right thing to do. He wrote, "'All things are lawful for me,' but not all things are helpful" (ESV). Or, as is commonly said by our grandmothers, "Just because you can, doesn't mean you should." Paul encouraged believers to ask themselves whether it would be helpful to do certain things. (In 1 Corinthians 10 Paul made this point again, and the word *helpful* is replaced by two words: *beneficial* and *constructive* [v. 23 NIV].)

When Paul wrote this he was speaking to a brewing controversy in the early church related to whether

Christians could eat leftover meat that was sacrificed to pagan gods (1 Cor. 8). Paul took the position of 1 Corinthians 6:12 on the issue. He said, "It's not an issue of whether it's right or wrong; it's an issue of whether it's helpful for you, and for your community, in your individual situation." In so many circumstances in my life, I've thought of this verse when I was deciding whether to do something. I don't ask myself whether something that seems amoral is "right or wrong," but whether it would be "helpful" if I did it. Then I err on the side of caution.

In Proverbs 16:9 Solomon cuts the balance between the decisions of man and the will of God. Solomon would have told Emily to just make a choice between any of the three job offers and rest assured that God would work with her plans to "establish" her steps. This is what God does. He doesn't lord over us like the pagan concept of God, but comes alongside us, as he originally did with Adam and Eve in the garden of Eden.

The Christian God is a God who desires a relationship with his people. He is not a God who takes pride in subjecting his people to his wrath, power, and judgment. This is why Jesus said, "This is eternal life: that they know you, the only true God" (John 17:3 NIV). Eternal life isn't just about spending eternity in heaven; it's about living in a right and enjoyable relationship with God right now. God's primary concern isn't our walking in step with his list of rules and regulations, but in our enjoyment of the life he created us to live. Not to endure life, but to really live, and to enjoy it.

When we make decisions on our own based upon the advice God has left us in his Word and gives us through prayer, we make God smile. We make him proud. We demonstrate that we appreciate the capacity he has given us and that we haven't taken for granted the wisdom he has made available to us.

THE WAY OF WISDOM VERSUS THE WAY OF REVELATION

Dr. Garry Friesen, in his exceptional book *Decision Making and the Will of God*, argues that there have been two predominant approaches to the will of God in church history. The first approach, which he calls the "way of wisdom," has been the predominant view in church history for hundreds upon hundreds of years. The second approach, which I call "the way of revelation," is a rather recent development, and while it is the most prominent view of our time, it hasn't always been that way.

The "way of wisdom" encapsulates much of what I've been writing in this book. It's a view of the will of God that infers that man has great autonomy in his decision making; that there isn't a bull's-eye to hit, but a lifestyle to live. It leaves the opportunity to take one of many forks in the road, and infers that man is responsible for taking the wisdom God has given him, and revealed in his Word, and applying it to all kinds of life situations.

The "way of revelation," on the other hand, involves the supernaturalizing of every step of decision making, and the inferred pressure to hit the bull's-eye, lest you "miss the will of God for your life." It is "waiting till God starts you" instead of "going till he stops you."

I think the "way of wisdom" is a more biblical approach, and have included an entire appendix in this book to further summarize Dr. Friesen's argument. For now, let's assume you agree with me and, if so, I think you'll appreciate these four guidelines given to us by Dr. Friesen to help us follow the "way of wisdom" in the difficult decisions of our life. They are:

1. Where God commands, we must obey.
2. Where there is no command, God gives us freedom.
3. Where this is no command, God gives us wisdom.
4. When we have chosen what is moral and wise, we must trust the sovereign God to work all the details together for good.[1]

We have to first accept that God's commands are binding on us as his children. They require our obedience, and we do so because they are right but also out of our love and affection for the God who gave them to us. This is the foundation for any reliance on his will for our lives. But occasionally we face a situation where there is no specific command to obey, and, to the relief of all those suffering from "decision paralysis," God gives us freedom to choose and to act.

The freedom God gives to us is predicated on the fact that we are already following him, seeking to know his character, and trying to understand his ways; but beyond this, we have the ability to choose whatever we think is best. God does not give us trick questions or lead us to a dead-end fork in the road. Rather, God will give us the wisdom to make a decision and the freedom to choose our path. This wisdom might take the form of a greater understanding of our own passions and personality. It might come on the other side of an honest conversation about what will truly make us happy, or it might come from an objective analysis of where each path will ultimately lead us. In all circumstances, God's promises serve as our safety net for he has already said that he "works for the good of those who love him, who have been called according to his purpose" (Rom. 8:28 NIV)—which even includes those decisions that, in the end, prove to have been misguided or less than ideal.

You're not going to be able to avoid making difficult decisions in your life.

Life is full of choices—thousands of them—and every single one of them has consequences. God designed it this way.

There's no use in fighting against it.

Rather, you must learn to manage these difficult, and inevitable, decisions.

We really get ourselves in trouble when we decide to not decide and delay the inevitable indefinitely, forcing ourselves to live in the in-between of life. We also get ourselves into trouble when we fail to realize that every decision we make has consequences, good and bad, and we fail to discipline ourselves to consider what could come from the decisions we make.

Too many people I know are living their lives crippled by indecision. This is a horrible way to live; it robs God of the glory he deserves for making you as he has. Sometimes you just have to make a choice, and then make it a good one.

God doesn't dislike it when you take this leadership of your own life. Rather, it makes him smile that you're using the freedom and wisdom he's worked so hard to make available to you.

He loves to see us taking what he's given us and doing something good with it, and when you face the forks in life's roads, rest assured you're not going to destroy your life with one decision.

Because you can't miss the will of God.

SIX

FINDING THE DEFIBRILLATOR

The role of prayer, sacrifice, and faith

THESE DAYS, IT SEEMS THERE ISN'T AN UNPUBLISHED idea out there—few keep their opinions to themselves anymore. People don't hesitate to log in and quickly shoot their thoughts and reactions into cyberspace, no matter the topic and whether—or not—they know anything about it. I could generally judge how controversial a visiting guest speaker was at Liberty University by the amount of e-mails that flooded my inbox. One of the more controversial speakers we ever had at Liberty University's weekly convocation—which is attended by more than ten thousand students—was someone who was speaking in ways I am now about the will of God. I'll keep the speaker nameless here, but let's just say people lost their minds, thinking that this way of thinking puts man too much at the center of God's plan and discounts the importance of prayer, sacrifice, and faith.

"How, after all," a student named James asked me, "can you say prayer is important to you if you're discouraging us from prayerfully waiting on God in our decision making? You're telling us to jump before we pray, and I just don't think that's right."

When I speak about how we must assert our God-given ability to make decisions, and how in making those decisions we find God's will for our lives, it's inevitable that some will accuse me of ignoring—or at least diminishing the importance of—the role of one's devotional life in decision making and the will of God. This isn't the case at all, but I want to explain this point a little more thoroughly.

In reality, the role of prayer, faith, and sacrifice (several key attributes of Christianity) isn't a peripheral issue when it comes to this approach to God's will—on the contrary, it is at the very heart of our faith in every sense, especially when it comes to discerning the will of God. The people who follow the approach highlighted in this book aren't the least spiritual and most pragmatic people—they should actually be the most spiritual. They should have a life so steadily planted on the foundation of God's Word, so focused on God's mission for them, that their decisions are inherently guarded against the self-centered distractions that threaten to derail their pursuit of God. They should be so focused on God that their will is conformed to his, almost naturally. This is another reason why I say that the will of God is more about *who* you are than about where you are or what you do in your life. The *who* that God wants you to be is not contingent on life circumstances, vocation, the school you're attending, or the place you're living. If you work on *who* you are, then much of *where you are* and *what you're doing* will take care of themselves.

People who embrace a revelatory approach to God's will, those who would encourage you to wait to "hear from God" before moving, are people whose approach is often based upon prayer, sacrifice, and faith. No serious Christian would question the importance of these characteristics, yet there is debate about how they play into God's will. I believe their chief contribution to your finding and following the will of God is related to their work in making *who you are*, making you the type of person who can submit your will to his, and I think this is true in very specific ways.

Just as an athlete is only fit to run the race after subjecting himself to a sufficiently rigorous training regiment, so is the believer only fit to exercise his God-given mind when that mind and will have been submitted to God through spiritual disciplines. Prayer, reading Scripture, and fasting are things that you do for your own sake, not to curry favor with God but to help you clearly understand his character and make you receptive to the plans he has for your life. Since you're supposed to mature in your faith as you gain more and more life experience, your growth ought to parallel the increasingly complex decisions of your life. As you get older and face more difficult decisions, you ought to have the compounded benefit of growing in your faith through other preceding decisions. The more decisions you make, the more you're prepared to make bigger ones and the more you'll understand the process that leads you to making a decision when you come to another crossroads.

This is what Solomon had in mind when he wrote in Proverbs 3:6, "In all your ways acknowledge Him, and He shall direct your paths" (NKJV). There was something natural in Solomon's admonition, something intuitive. He was essentially saying, "Just work on becoming the person God wants you to be, and God will take care of guiding you." He was not writing with the attitude of one begging and pleading for God to tell him to take this job or that job or live in this place or that place. It's much more lighthearted than that. He was essentially saying, "Keep your heart pure and God will take care of the rest." It's the same attitude (or theology!) that Solomon presented in Proverbs 16:9: "A man's heart plans his way, but the LORD directs his steps" (NKJV). If it sounds simple, it's supposed to be. He's almost telling us: "Relax, chill out, and stop putting so much pressure on yourself. You just work on *you* and God will take care of the rest."

Your spiritual disciplines make you, and then you make decisions. God invites himself into the process whenever he likes to shore up your way or to stop you from going in a particular direction.

PRAYER KEEPS OUR HEARTS CLOSE TO GOD

Every time I pray, I am acknowledging God's supremacy and my own inadequacy. Prayer is an exercise in humility that forces me to subject my own will to God's. You don't pray to God as a peer. You pray to God as one inferior to him. The regular practice of prayer has the effect of keeping your ego at bay, and keeping your heart in a place of submission to the Almighty. Regular prayer has the effect of building spiritual priorities into the rhythm of your everyday life.

When I think of prayer, I am touched by the story of German pastor Martin Rinkart, who buried nearly five thousand fellow townsmen and church members, including his wife, all in one year during the Thirty Years' War. He would conduct up to fifty funerals a day. His shoulders must have been sore from digging so many graves, his mind weak from conducting so many services. His

church was ruined by war, disease, and financial difficulty, yet one night he wrote this prayer of hope from the
heart of despair:

Now thank we all our God
With heart and hands and voices;
Who wondrous things hath done,
In whom this world rejoices.
Who, from our mother's arms,
Hath led us on our way
With countless gifts of love
And still is ours today.

O may this bounteous God
Through all our life be near us,
With ever joyful hearts
And blessed peace to cheer us;
And keep us still in grace,
And guide us when perplexed;
And free us from all ills,
In this world and the next.[1]

The apostle Paul made a radical statement about
the priority prayer must have in your life, a statement
that Pastor Rinkart surely understood: "pray without
ceasing" (1 Thess. 5:17 NKJV). Paul was not just talking about a spiritual discipline that you should practice

with regularity. He was talking about a way of living that hinges upon prayer, with prayer as its anchor and its heart. You pray as you breathe. Your default reaction to any number of circumstances in your daily life is to pray. Prayer becomes the musical score adding beauty to your day. It becomes a part of who you are, not just something you do.

You are spiritually impaired in making good decisions if you aren't regularly praying to God. (This isn't a book about prayer, but there are plenty of good ones out there. Read all of them you can find—start with E. M. Bounds—and then begin to pray more than you already do until you get to a place in your life when you almost pray without thinking.)

SACRIFICE KEEPS OUR HEARTS PURE FOR GOD

God's plan for your life will always involve some form of sacrifice. Sacrifice is at the heart of Christianity, it's at the heart of the gospel, and it should be at the heart of a life lived in submission to God's will. Some people, when faced with a fork in the road, will decide to take the path that requires the least resistance and the least sacrifice. That may or may not be the best decision based upon your particular situation, but if you are deciding simply to do, or not do, something because you don't want to enter into a season or a challenge that might require sacrifice, then you are making a decision dangerously.

God's expectation is that his followers are willing to sacrifice. He goes so far as to say that the Christian life ought to be, in itself, a lifestyle of sacrifice (Rom. 12:1). The Bible tells us that we ought to be willing to sacrifice what we have for others (Heb. 13:16), and the entire Old Testament (and much of the New Testament) is based upon the sacrificial system instituted by God with Abraham in Genesis. This isn't just a theological point—the church has been at its best in history when it has been willing to sacrifice. There are myriad stories of early Christians sacrificing their wealth, their opportunities, their homes, their futures, and even their lives so that others would benefit from that sacrifice.

Scripture places great emphasis on sacrifice, especially in regards to money. In the Old Testament God instituted a system of "tithing" that required his people give 10 percent of their income, regardless of their status in society. The New Testament church had a reputation for giving even more, such that anti-Christian political leaders couldn't help but recognize their generosity. The Roman emperor Julian famously wrote in a letter to a friend, "(Christianity) has been specially advanced through the loving service rendered to strangers, and through their care for the burial of the dead. It is a scandal that there is not a single Jew who is a beggar, and that the godless Galileans care not only for their own poor but for ours as well; while those who belong to us look in vain for the help that we should render them."[2] It was even common among the early Christians for lower-class families to sacrifice meals so that they could provide food for families who were even less fortunate.

This is why Scripture uses aggressive terminology in warning of the dangers of loving money. If you're not willing to sacrifice money, or anything else, then your heart is already polluted by a value system that could adversely affect your decision making. In my own life, and in the lives of people I've worked with, I've noticed that one of the first signs of spiritual sickness is an unwillingness to consider sacrificing something. Nothing unveils one's values system more clearly than this. It shows clearly that you've been bound by the world's values, and once you are so bound it is incredibly difficult to shake off those chains. C. S. Lewis wrote, "Prosperity knits a man to the World. He feels he is 'finding his place in it,' while it is really finding its place in him."[3]

FAITH KEEPS OUR HEARTS RELIANT ON GOD

Frankly, I don't like that Jesus puts faith at the heart of Christianity. I don't like that Hebrews 11:6 says "without faith it is impossible to please God" (NIV), and I especially don't like that God intentionally challenges us in this area. I've known people of extraordinary faith and have even been fortunate to be mentored by a number of them, but faith remains hard for me. People who walk confidently into the future, with no clue of what's in front of them, are inspirations to me, but I have a hard time living this way myself. I know this already, and because of this I know that I will always be tempted to make decisions of least resistance in this area. I'll be tempted to pick the choice that doesn't require me to step out in faith, while simultaneously admiring those who do.

Yet faith is God's primary means of keeping his children reliant upon him. It forces us to put ourselves in situations where we can't take care of ourselves, and requires that we apply the truth that we say we believe. Nothing strengthens our spiritual lives more, but nothing is more challenging.

Faith grows through taking steps of confidence, and chooses an attitude of optimism when everything seems to discourage it. Faith is required in nearly every moment of significant change in life, and God requires more faith when you're ready for it. Faith challenges you to flex your spiritual muscles beyond what you think you can bear, but God knows what you're capable of bearing. He never gives you a challenge too big, even though you think it might be. Each of us, at some point in our lives, will have to close our eyes and take a leap. Our challenge is taking the leap; it's God who steps in to catch us and carry us back down to solid ground.

God requires faith in our lives because he believes in us entirely, and he knows we have more spiritual grit in us than we think we have. So, he presses us. He forces us to challenge ourselves so that we realize that we have more in us than we thought we had.

We think that faith puts us in a needy and vulnerable place, but we can be encouraged knowing that in reality, God requires faith from us as the first indication that we're stronger than we think we are and that we're ready for bigger things.

BEING HONEST WITH YOURSELF

When someone you know well is having a hard time but refuses to acknowledge it, you might ask them, "How are you *really*?" You add emphasis to that final word to imply that you actually know—simply by looking at them—that they are holding something back. I'm not sure why we refuse to be honest about our condition sometimes. It must go to the heart of our age-old battle for control, all the way back to the garden of Eden, when man tried to assert his own will over God's. To this day we tend to buck up and put on a show when everything is actually falling apart.

Sometimes this battle gets so out of control that we begin to lie to ourselves. I remember a particularly dark and difficult season I went through in my own spiritual walk. My relationship with God had been on the rocks for a long time. My love for the Word of God had been reduced to a need-to-know type of relationship that only took me to the Bible when I needed something—or worse, needed to teach someone something. The most troubling part of this experience was when I realized that I was lying to myself. I was telling myself that I was better off than I actually was, and when a good friend would question my relationship with God, I would immediately jump into a carefully practiced self-defense. I would argue convincingly that everything was okay. Sometimes, it was as if I was even trying to convince myself. My soul was nearly depleted of its spiritual life, and rather than fess up, I lied to myself and to others.

I did this enough that I actually began to believe it, even as my spiritual life spiraled into a deeper and darker hole. Eventually I was so deeply broken that I didn't have the strength to pull myself out, even when I would get a rare glimpse into my genuine need to straighten up my relationship with God. A lot of time passed between my growing realization of how spiritually troubled I was and my ability to actually do something about it. I realized my problem and wanted to change it long before I was able to do so. All of this was because my self-deception and defensiveness had starved my soul. I didn't need to get healthy again—I needed to be made alive again. It took a great work of the Holy Spirit during a time of great change and great challenge before I had the strength to practice my spiritual disciplines again and before my faith came back to life.

If you can, don't let yourself get into that kind of a dark place. Instead, pray, sacrifice with intentionality, and walk with a straight back and confident stare into the challenges required by faith. It's better that way. It keeps your own will at bay, and it prepares you to move forward into life's different seasons with confidence in your God because of the confidence you have in your relationship with him. Because the alternative is an egregious form of pride that asserts your own authority over God's and so thoroughly embraces self-deception that you actually think you can walk through this life alone.

A Christian who doesn't pray, isn't willing to sacrifice, and devalues faith is a Christian whose spiritual life has been injected with the same disease of pride that caused Satan himself to rebel against the Almighty. In this way, there is no in-between. There is no middle ground to negotiate.

A Christian who doesn't pray is a Christian who actually believes he does not need God. A Christian who doesn't sacrifice is one who really thinks that what she has is her own. A Christian who rejects faith is one who really thinks that Jesus was lying. While I don't believe you ought to wait around praying for God's will while he has already given you so many gifts, passions, and opportunities, I also believe that you should be a person of great prayer, great sacrifice, and great faith. If you're anything less, then you have more in common with Satan than you do with Jesus.

That's a hard truth, but it's truth I had to face myself. Maybe it's a truth you need to face too.

SEVEN

THE CRAZY GUY WITH AN UMBRELLA IN THE DALAI LAMA'S TOWN

Learning to live aware

FROM ITS INCEPTION, CHRISTIANITY HAS ALWAYS HAD an integrative approach to life. Christianity was not meant to be compartmentalized or cooped up in church sanctuaries. It was meant to be fully and comprehensively transformative, from the inside out, and it was meant to be lived out in the world. It was meant to affect the whole person and the whole world as that person moved through his or her everyday life.

Christ didn't aim to create people who simply practiced spiritual disciplines or went to church on Sundays, but to create people who were entirely different from the world around them. He aimed to help people discover who they were really meant to be. This began with him, on the cross, opening the door into the opportunity for this transformation and has continued for centuries as generations have attempted to live Christlike lives.

In Christianity we don't carve up the segments of life into those parts of us that are more spiritual and those that are more secular. On the contrary, we see it all as one. Everything is holy to the Christian, and everything is for God's glory and to contribute to Jesus' Great Commission. When you start to live this way, start to recognize the holy in the everyday, then you begin to have a Christian experience that is much more exciting. You start to see the hand of God at work in your life in really, really remarkable ways. You begin to see how God is more regularly interjecting himself into your story and bringing about divine encounters and preparing you for future opportunities and challenges.

Sometimes when people consider the approach to God's will that I'm advocating in this book, they view it as a less mysterious way of interacting with God. It seems much more interesting to follow the other path. However, I believe quite the contrary. I believe that you see and experience the hand of God in your life in much more profound ways when you recognize more fully that life is you and God working together, and not simply you wandering through the world with the expectation that God is going to make decisions for you, answer all your questions, and show you the next step.

Life is you and God, together. He authorizes you to make decisions, and then he steps in and weaves those decisions into a glorious tapestry depicting his goodness and grace. When you start to think of your life this way, then you start to live aware of what's happening around you. You begin asking yourself whether the conversation you're having with the stranger you just met is a divine encounter or whether the moments of life that seem coincidental are actually miraculous. Walking down the street becomes an adventure; sitting next to a stranger on the bus becomes a chance to change someone's life. You start looking for God's divine hand in your everyday life, and when you start looking you start realizing that God is anything but silent.

He's ever present. He's always up to something.

THE GUY WITH THE UMBRELLA

In each of my previous books, I've written about my experiences in India, including multiple visits I have made to the Himalayan village in India the Dalai Lama calls home. It was there, in the Dalai Lama's city, that I first became "aware."

Each morning I made a trek to the Dalai Lama's

temple to have my own devotions. I sat on a crumbling old step and read my Bible and prayed as I watched elderly Buddhists make their daily circles and prostrations at this particularly auspicious place. The temple looks about how you would expect it to look. It sits on the top of a high hill with a bird's-eye view of the lower Himalayan Mountains. There are various spaces of worship, indoors and out. There are bells ringing and the smell of incense intoxicates the air. The wind whips crazily around the mountains, causing the Tibetan prayer flags, which are hanging everywhere, to start flapping wildly with this popping noise that echoes through the mountains. It's an otherworldly place. It's a place where you'd expect the Dalai Lama to live.

One morning I had decided I would read through the entire book of Acts in one sitting. With renewed eyes I read page after page, sitting among worshipping Buddhists in an entirely Buddhist city. It gave me a powerful sense of what it must have been like for the apostles to preach the gospel in such an entirely non-Christian environment. I saw their boldness differently, I saw how the power of their miracles turned people's attention to Jesus, and I was confronted deep in my heart to live for Christ more boldly.

In particular I was challenged by a story in Acts about a demon-possessed person the apostles encountered. The guy was clearly considered the "town crazy," and surely everyone knew who he was. Then God healed him in the middle of the city through the power of Jesus at the hands of his apostles. As I read that story with new eyes, it suddenly made sense to me how at that time entire communities would convert to Christ. The disciples were doing crazy things, living for Christ in crazy ways, and when the demon-possessed, crazy man walked up to them, they cast the demon out of him and his changed life gathered the attention of everyone in town.

I sat on that step and imagined what would happen in that village if God worked in this powerful way. The village had one little square in its center, and all the activity took place there. If a miracle of this kind happened in this place, then the eyes of the entire city would be turned to Christ. My heart was breaking as I watched the Buddhists around me worship and as I prayed through my own lack of faith. I asked myself, "God, would I have the courage of the disciples to act immediately in your name if I had such an opportunity to show your power in this city?"

That afternoon it happened.

I had just finished lunch in the village square when an insane man came running and screaming at me with an umbrella. The whole thing happened in what seemed like slow motion. He wasn't just running in my direction. He was running *at* me with his umbrella pointed at me like a sword. By the reaction of the locals standing around, it seemed as if this behavior wasn't unexpected from this particular man. Now, it's at this point that the story is supposed to get interesting, right? I'm supposed to tell you that I rose up in boldness, harkening back to the scriptures I had read only a few hours earlier, and I called down fire from heaven and converted the guy in plain sight of everyone looking around.

That would have been great.

That's not what happened.

Instead, I dodged the guy's umbrella.

I went walking the other way, and to this day I ask myself what could have happened in that moment had I been more aware.

It was creepy how absolutely identical the situation I faced there was to the situation described in the scriptures I had read that morning. It really opened my eyes to try to pay attention to what God is doing around me, and it's amazing how often I see his hand. In fact, I just saw it a few minutes ago.

I'm typing this chapter in a discreet upstairs corner of a small coffee shop near my home. It's late at night. I'm all by myself. I'm not that recognizable. I'm wearing a baseball cap and facing the wall. Yet, moments ago, a young Rwandan student came up to me to tell me about his life's vision and his experiences in Africa, and he told me about how his parents are doing significant work in the Sudan.

I told him how I had just come from Rwanda a few

days ago, and how I spent some time there strategizing about how we could use Rwanda as a launching pad to reach people in the Sudan since the Sudan has hundreds of ethnic groups that are entirely unreached.

Coincidence? Hardly.

Divine encounter? Certainly.

BECOMING AWARE

What does it mean to be aware? It means that you expect God to be at the heart of the unexpected and you look for the twist of Providence in everyday moments. God is doing this sort of thing all the time. We're just not paying attention.

As I'm writing there is an Iranian-American pastor who has been imprisoned in Iran's most notorious prison for more than a year because of his Christian faith. His wife, Nagmeh, who has been pleading for his release, came to Liberty University, where she spoke to ten thousand students in the basketball arena. She told the story of the faithfulness of her husband and we asked our students to pray. Nagmeh then boarded a flight to New York City to attend the United Nations General Assembly's annual meeting. She was hoping to put pressure on the international body to secure the release of her husband. Nagmeh was sitting in the lobby of her hotel when Iran's president walked through the lobby. At that moment she happened to be carrying a letter for the president, and she was able to hand deliver it to him.

Do you think that was a coincidence? Of course it wasn't. God was wrapping history around that moment, and had been moving chess pieces for a thousand years to arrange that precise encounter at that precise time. He's kind like that, and he's careful about it too.

Hopefully, by the time this book releases, God will have checkmated the Iranian government and arranged the release of Nagmeh's husband, Saeed. But if he doesn't, it's probably also a part of a thousand-year plan. Because God is never surprised.

SO MUCH MORE

The church has said for centuries that God works in "strange and mysterious ways." The Bible is filled with the stories and testimonies of Christians who've lived their Christian lives to the fullest and seen the amazing, subtle, and profound ways in which God has worked.

I am convinced that God has more in store for most of our lives than we think. He is not just interested in us; he is actively at work in our lives in truly profound ways. You just need to be aware, and then ask him sometimes to remind you of how he's working in your life. I did that just this morning. There are a few things on my mind that are burdening me. I have some unanswered questions and unmet needs and I'm confused about a few things. So today I've asked him to step into my story. I've asked him to intervene in a way that only he can, and to show me once again that he's at the heart of it all, whether I sense his presence or not.

God is intervening all the time. He's doing it in profound and powerful ways, sometimes in ways that are apparent to you and sometimes in ways that are less obvious. It's here that we find the mystery of our faith. I wish I could give you a formula that you could apply to recognize his hand at work, but it doesn't work this way. It's like love. You don't quite know how to love, but you know when you do.

That's how the *aware* lifestyle is lived—it's a by-product of your growing and deepening relationship with God, and your relationship with God is deepened by the exercise of your own will under the submission of God's greater will. Then adventure comes, and there's plenty of it to be had.

THE EXPERIMENT

Why don't you do today, at this very moment, what I did this morning? Why don't you ask God to make you aware as you're moving forward on your planned and expected path? Why don't you spend the rest of the day asking yourself whether every conversation, every chance encounter, every surprise is actually something greater? Ask whether God is shoring up your steps, and ask yourself what chess move this might be and how it might play into God's cosmic plan.

God designed the universe with every action affecting every other action in a way that the insignificant moments of life can work out profound changes as the dominoes of history fall. It's what scientists call the "butterfly effect"—how the flapping of a butterfly's wings on one continent can be the spark that results in a hurricane on another. Every day, you are playing a significant and meaningful role in a truly profound story. There is no such thing as an insignificant moment.

Every moment is divine. We need only be aware.

PART 2

HOW CAN I STAY COMMITTED TO GOD'S WILL FOR MY LIFE?

EIGHT

KILLED TWICE FOR A BIBLE

How commitment is the secret to success

Too often we blame the ambiguity of God's will for our inaction. We say, "I just don't know what God wants for my life," and use that as an excuse for continuing wherever we are, stuck. And some of us, whether we realize it or not, even blame God for our difficult seasons in life, in essence saying it is God's silence that is condemning us to indecision. So we shift responsibility to God and continue to do whatever is most comfortable for us, missing out on the freedom and rewards of choice.

I believe the remedy for this is to get moving. To pull yourself up by your bootstraps, to take the hands and feet and the good brain that God has given you and get moving in the most logical direction toward your life's goal—and to be committed. See, more often than not, when people complain about how difficult it is to "find God's will," they don't realize that the real difficulty isn't finding it, but being committed to it. Because though it's easy to find, it's difficult to stick to.

COMMITMENT ISSUES

There's a reason why it's so common in our culture today to speak of commitment issues. Ever since Freud began to theorize about the inner workings of the human mind, the phrase "fear of commitment" has been branded into our brains. We are taught almost to expect that we will be unable to commit to things (such as relationships, careers, New Year's resolutions, etc.) in the long term. To say that we struggle with commitment is a profound understatement.

Every single person I know struggles with commitment at times. It seems there's something inherently broken inside of us that makes it difficult for us to stick to whatever we've started. We have a hard time just staying in one place, doing one thing, for any period of time. And what are the results? Shallow faith, weak relationships, short attention spans, more stress, lack of stability in family life, poor physical health, and bad work ethic, among others. The results are all bad, but it seems we don't learn our lesson. We just climb right back on the hamster wheel and take another twirl.

Yet those who do manage to commit: emplyees who stay with the same company for a decade or more, pastors who lead the same church for years, or students who stick with the same program of study—are almost always better off for their "stick-to-it-iveness." This has been my own professional experience. While I personally struggle with commitment as much as anyone, I worked for Liberty University for more than a dozen years. A reporter, who recently interviewed me about some of the remarkable experiences I've had in my professional life, asked, "As a young leader, what is your secret to success?"

My answer wasn't profound. I simply said, "I had the same job for more than a decade. It's amazing what you can accomplish if you pick one place and one goal and just stick to it for a long haul."

This is true in circumstance after circumstance. I believe you're always better off if you just stay where you are a little while, yet this is one of the least practiced disciplines of our time. I can't begin to tell you how many twentysomethings I've known or counseled who have had multiple jobs in multiple states between college graduation and their thirtieth birthdays. They've played fast and loose with their future by jumping from one opportunity to the next without considering the value of staying in one place long enough to realize success. If you think I am exaggerating, a survey quoted in *Forbes* found that 91 percent of millennials expect to be at their current job for less than three years.[1] The term *job-hopping* has come to describe these people who move from job to job and never settle down. They become discouraged when their goals have not been accomplished, and they wonder what they're doing wrong, so instead of working harder to fit in, they leave. (As I am writing this, I am grateful Steve Jobs didn't stop after three years.)

There are reasons why we have this tendency and we'll discuss those reasons a little later, but for now it's important to understand that if you're attempting to follow God's will, you're not going to do much unless you work diligently on becoming a more committed person. Without question, history's most influential personalities have—at their very cores—been people of immovable commitment.

COMMITMENT EMBODIED

William Tyndale is a good example of a person of deep commitment. He had degrees from Oxford and Cambridge, was a professor of Greek, and was well versed in classical languages. For someone who lived in the fifteenth century, you can't imagine a better-educated person. He would have definitely been voted "most likely to succeed." He was the embodiment of a European aristocrat with a mind that could have made him rich and famous, but William Tyndale was also a deeply committed Christian who believed he had a greater contribution to make to the world than his own personal success.

Tyndale was passionate about making the Bible accessible to the masses, prying it from the hands of the educational elites and the priests whom he felt had monopolized the book. He imagined a world where every person could read the Bible in a language they understood. At some point in his life, he realized he had both a vision and the skills to bring that vision to fruition. Like Paul, he was made for the job.

Inspired by Martin Luther's theology, Tyndale began the hugely controversial task of translating the Bible from Latin into English, the language of the people, so that "even the commonest farmer" could read the Bible without a priest serving as its intermediary. At first he tried to recruit the support of the British clergy, but he was immediately rebuffed as a heretic and radical. The religious leaders believed that translating the Bible out of Latin, the "church language," was an act of irreverence, and they believed that this type of transgression justified the most severe punishment. Tyndale eventually had to flee to Germany, where he met Martin Luther and shared with him his ideas about translating Scripture.

At no point did Tyndale lose his vision. He worked tenaciously, despite the threat of death and a torrent of opposition, and he finished his task in 1525 in Worms, Germany, with the publication of the Tyndale Bible. When copies of the Tyndale Bible were smuggled into England, it caused an enormous uproar. The books were burned in the streets, Tyndale was reviled for his heresy, or even insanity, and his life's work was treated with disdain. Eventually, King Henry VIII executed William Tyndale, and as an added insult, they burned his body.

Tyndale died for his work, but never for a moment did he lose his vision and his commitment to make the Bible available to the everyday man. His Bible became the foundation for countless other Bible translations. Some estimates suggest 76 percent and 83 percent of the King James Version's Old and New Testaments are actually from Tyndale's Bible. The grandchildren of those who killed Tyndale would be the ones treating him as a biblical scholar! Tyndale became an inspiration to generations of Christians who have stood stalwart in the face of the most ardent opposition in order to accomplish whatever it was that God called them to do. Tyndale died in shame to the world, but as a hero to the faith.[2]

William Tyndale would have never made such a difference if he weren't committed, and millions of people around the world wouldn't have enjoyed the blessing of having the Bible in their own languages. Undoubtedly

we can all agree to honor and commend Tyndale's contribution, yet we discount in our own lives the very thing
that made such a contribution possible—commitment.
William Tyndale's lifestyle of commitment didn't begin
when he embarked on translating the Bible; it must have
started much earlier. If he hadn't been a committed person, he wouldn't have been able to master the languages
required to translate the Bible. It must have begun when
he was a student at Oxford, struggling through learning Greek, or when he first realized that the servant who
brought him his breakfast in the morning was as igno-
rant of Scripture as if God had never sent his own Word
to enlighten mankind. Otherwise he would never have
been able to follow through with such a colossal task,
much less under the pressure of full-scale opposition
from both the government and the church. Tyndale was
a man who cultivated this commitment in his life so that
it was there when he needed it.

We see in William Tyndale the principle that those
who find success are those preparing themselves when
no one is looking. The kind of commitment that holds up
under intense pressure is fostered in doing homework in
college, in making choices to use your time as you should
and not necessarily as you want to. It comes in making
yourself get up half an hour earlier in the morning to
spend time with God and in going to the gym after work
when all you want is to veg out on your couch at home. It's

fostered in moments where you want to open your mouth in wrath, but choose instead to be a person of peace. It's found when you are exhausted but have one more goal in mind for the day, so you press on through, realizing later that you had more in you than you thought.

C. S. Lewis once wrote about the importance of everyday choices: "Every time you make a choice you are turning the central part of you, the part of you that chooses, into something a little different than it was before."[3] We have the ability to make ourselves into people of great commitment to the faith and to God's will for our lives, and that transformation starts with the choices that may seem insignificant in the moment. In reality, these could be the choices that turn the course of history in a different direction.

If you want the type of commitment that changes history, then cultivate it in little decisions every day—maybe even the decision to finish this book?

NINE

FEARING LOSS AND KILLING ANIMALS

What is commitment really?

ELIZABETH GURNEY WAS BORN ON MAY 21, 1780, IN Norfolk, England, to a family of devout Quakers who were devoted to the development of their children's minds and the cultivation of their hearts. Elizabeth was read on the works of Mary Wollstonecraft and Thomas Paine, and was sufficiently mature by the time she was twelve years old to care for her brothers and sisters after the tragic death of her mother. Maybe it was this experience that sensitized her to words of the famous Quaker preacher William Savery, whom she heard preach when she was eighteen years old. As he argued forcefully that it was the duty of all Christians to alleviate the poverty and suffering of the masses, his words pierced Elizabeth to the core.

This message and its call wedged deep into Elizabeth's heart, and it sat there for many years while she married, had eleven children of her own, and strove to be for her new family what her mom's tragic death made impossible for her own. Then, in 1812, the burden on her heart became unbearable. On a tear-stained page of her journal, she wrote that her life was "slipping away to no purpose." She knew that the burden she had borne since hearing William Savery was at risk of being suppressed so entirely that her heart would no longer be moved by it, and she absolutely had to act on this burden before she lost her purpose for living.

So she did.

Through the influence of another Quaker, Stephen Grellet, she began to work with the female inmates of Newgate prison. These ladies, along with their children, were crammed into an inadequate space with little sanitation, no bedding or clothing, and not enough food. So Elizabeth established the Association for the Improvement of Female Prisoners in Newgate and began to bring food, clothing, and blankets to the prisoners. She eventually became the first woman to ever be called before the House of Commons (in order to testify about the condition of the prisoners in Newgate), and, in the end, her committed work resulted in massive reforms to the prison system. Hundreds of lives were affected by her kindness, and more than one thousand people attended her funeral.[1]

One sermon placed one burden on her heart and, later, when life had long overwhelmed that burden, Elizabeth became fearful of forgetting it. So she acted, urgently and decisively, and stayed committed until the very end. She found her purpose and, in turn, gave help and hope to thousands. She knew what God's will was for her life, but she eventually had to commit herself to fulfilling it.

WHAT IS COMMITMENT?

Commitment researchers would not be surprised by Elizabeth's story, and that Elizabeth's fear of losing her purpose emboldened her to act on a once-weak conviction and turn it into a commitment that would change thousands of lives.

In fact, commitment is, at its core, motivated by the fear of loss. You can fear losing many different things —a job, an opportunity, a goal, a purpose, your relationship with God, your spouse or a friend—but it is this fear of loss that motivates you to hold on when you want to give in, to press through when you want to give up, and to believe that it is worth whatever sacrifice is required to stay true to the end. At your core, you believe that breaking that commitment would cause harm; whether it harms you, someone you care about, or the world you're living in.

When you start to look at commitment through this lens, then you start to understand how your commitments fail, and why you sometimes struggle with commitment issues. Social scientists tell us that the power of commitment is in one's perception of the consequences that would result from breaking it. Once the fear of loss is matched or exceeded by the difficulties of maintaining our commitment, we may feel that it has become too hard to keep going, and we will give up. So if you come to a point in a relationship where breaking a commitment (whether it is to a spouse or to a friend) no longer seems like it will cause considerable harm, then it's easier to break that commitment. On the contrary, if breaking a commitment will cause more damage than maintaining it, we will be more motivated to commit. For example, if you're in an unhappy marriage, but you have children you dearly love, you might be compelled to hold on to your marriage in order to spare your children from harm.

Circumstances like these are where we really learn what is most important to us. If, for instance, you're going through a season of life where your faith isn't very important to you, then it becomes easier to make decisions that are harmful to your faith (or that cause further loss of your faith). If the Great Commission isn't important to you, then you won't be committed to opportunities to contribute to it. Why? Because you aren't fearful of losing your opportunity to be a part of it, or of the harm it might cause to you (or your life's purpose) by not having the Great Commission at the center of your life, or that some people who are lost might have heard of Jesus had you fulfilled your own call.

Your values—what's most important to you—must be planted deep inside of you and regularly nurtured in order for you to be able to stay committed to whatever God has for you.

TWO DIFFERENT KINDS OF COMMITMENT

Social scientists go even further by teaching us that there are two different kinds of commitment: commitment through coercion and commitment through dedication. Each is helpful, but the latter is more powerful.

Commitment through coercion (the weaker of the two) is the one we've already talked about. It's negative in its motivation. It pushes us into commitment by taking advantage of the fear of loss. It is coercive, not motivational. Let me give you an example: Let's say your doctor tells you that if you don't start exercising, you will have a high chance of developing heart disease or diabetes. So you start going to the gym. You aren't there because you are looking to have a fit body. You're not there because you're working on losing your belly and cutting a six-pack. You're not even there because you enjoy physical activity. You're only there because you're fearful of losing your life if you don't begin to exercise.

Here's another example: Let's say you made a commitment to a friend to help on a project. It's a huge project involving the full-scale remodeling of a part of their home. You didn't know all that was involved in the project when you made a half-hearted commitment to help over an informal lunch. You don't want to help. You're not sure you have the time or skills to help, but you decide, "Because I promised I'm going to do this, I'm just going to have to do it."

Do you notice the negative sense of motivation in each example? This can keep you committed for a little while, but it isn't the best form of motivation. It's the kind of commitment that will cave when your exercise regimen produces few results or when your friend's remodeling stretches into months rather than a weekend or two.

Commitment through dedication is more difficult to define, but it is far more powerful. This kind of commitment is built not on fear, but on hope. It looks forward to the accomplishment of a goal that outweighs any trouble or pain it will take to get there. This goal finds its roots in your identity and stems from who you believe you are and why you believe you're here. This goal is something you believe you were created to do, and to deny yourself the accomplishment of that goal is to deny the person God made you to be. You feel positive about this commitment because it means living up to your own sense of self. Commitment through coercion focuses entirely on fulfilling responsibility, but commitment through dedication encompasses passion in the performance of one's responsibility. The distinction in motivation may seem subtle, but it makes all the difference.

For example, a friend of mine was speaking to me the other day about her hobby—hunting. She absolutely loves to go hunting. None of her brothers got into hunting, so she decided to go along with her dad once, and ever since she has loved the sport. This is, of course, precarious to the man she'll marry one day because 1) she'll be a better shot than him, and 2) she can pick him off from way down the road if he ever decides to leave her.

When my friend talks about hunting, her eyes light up. It's not just something she is committed to because she doesn't want her dad to hunt alone—it's something she is passionate about. She told me about sitting in the deer stand for hours, just waiting for the moment a deer came within range. Now, in a deer stand, you can't talk or move very much. You just sit there, for hours, in anticipation. It's cold; your muscles stiffen and cramp from sitting on the hard metal seat. All you have to think about is the smell of the damp air or the occasional flutter of a bird in the tree. No cell phones. No distractions. Nothing to do but sit and wait.

For me, hunting sounds like torture, but to her it's the most wonderful thing in the world. She's not doing this because she has to; she is doing it because it's part of who she is and she enjoys it. I asked her how she could endure the anticipation and the hours of waiting. She said, "I know what I'm waiting for: that unmistakable rhythm of steps that signals the approach of a deer. Every sound makes your heart skip and your hands tighten around the stock of your gun, ready to raise it up to your shoulder and sight down the scope for a clean kill. That moment when the crosshairs align over a smooth tawny shoulder is an experience of perfect clarity, untouched by the chaos of the rest of your life. That is your goal." Can you sense the passion in her voice? This is what separates those who commit through dedication from those who commit through fear or coercion. They believe in something and they are passionate about whatever it is.

This isn't a book about solidifying your belief system, but what I can tell you is that your beliefs are grown like plants. Every belief begins with a seed that grows when properly nurtured. God has, through your conscience, planted most of the seeds already in your heart. If you nurture them the roots will grow deep, and as those beliefs flourish they will become your passion. And your commitments grow in the same soil as your beliefs; they are stalks on the same stem, sharing the same sunlight.

Becoming a person who is committed to whatever path you take in life is not a decision you make with a flip of a switch. It involves a certain awareness of your identity. It involves questions about who you think you are compared to who God says you are, what you believe, and what God says you should believe. (There are lots of great books that can help you with these questions, like C. S. Lewis's *Mere Christianity*, Watchman Nee's *The Normal Christian Life*, and Rick Warren's *The Purpose Driven Life*.)

Asking yourself these questions and exploring their answers is the secret to addressing your commitment issues, because the roots of these issues go down deep. And one thing is absolutely true: if we don't aggressively confront our commitment issues, we won't be able to fulfill the will of God in our lives as we could have had we focused on this part of who we are. The truth is that many of us wouldn't actually stick with God's will even if he spoke to us from a voice in heaven, because we don't know how to stay committed.

Commitment isn't easy, but it is possible and it is essential. Most of us think the answer to life is "knowing God's will," when it is actually learning to stay committed enough to live it.

TEN

SLAVES, NURSES, AND NAZIS

Why is commitment so important?

PHIL WAS TWENTY-SEVEN YEARS OLD. HE HAD UNDER-graduate and master's degrees in business, he was from a good family, he was bilingual, and he was the type of person who made friends instantly with almost everyone he met. He was the perfect picture of a potentially successful businessman. You couldn't have designed a more promising picture of a highly educated twentysomething ready to enter the business world. The guy even dressed like he had a personal stylist from *GQ*.

Yet Phil's story was just about the farthest thing from what you'd expect of such a talented young person.

Instead of entering into a major corporation right out of college with the intention of rising up in the company over time, Phil was on his fifth job in his fourth state. He hadn't spent more than eight months at any of his jobs, and his life was a wreck because of all the instability. And this wasn't just the case with his professional life—his personal life was also in shambles. He had had half a dozen different girlfriends and could never take any of those relationships to a serious place.

"I have commitment issues," he told me.

When I asked why, he said, "I don't know. I think it's just my personality."

And you know what? He was wrong. Research tells us that a person's ability to stay committed to a task, a person, a company—you name it—has nothing to do with his or her personality.[1] That means there isn't a single person on the planet who is, by their nature, incapable of living a committed life. It's not that they can't—it's that they choose not to, and that choice is easier or more difficult based upon what they *believe*, not who they *are*.

As I said in the last chapter, I believe that we must pay attention to and examine our commitment issues, because they have powerful ramifications on our faith, our work, our relationships, and our character. If we don't deal with this area of our life, we won't be able to follow God's will if we "find it."

OUR FAITH COMMANDS COMMITMENT

———

If something is true, then it requires your commitment. If you believe that the Bible is true, then its truth demands to be taken seriously. Our dedication to our faith and our obedience to the commands of Scripture lead us to commit to excellence in all other areas of our lives. We are called by our faith to commit to our work, and we are commanded by Scripture to build relationships that glorify God.

Our faith—our relationship with Christ—is our primary commitment, and the one to which we should direct the most energy. When we are secure in our faith, though we still encounter difficulties, we are completely confident in God's sovereignty and our own purpose. Faith and commitment go hand in hand because the currency of faith is truth, and truth emboldened by commitment is the most powerful thing in the world.

Take, for example, the story of Thomas Clarkson. Clarkson was born in Cambridgeshire, England, in 1760, the son of a preacher. He was brilliant from childhood and famously won an essay contest when he was nineteen years old. His essay, which was later published, was entitled "An Essay on Slavery and Commerce of the Human Species." The essay attracted and inspired some of the most famous abolitionists in England, including William Wilberforce.

While not nearly as well-known as Wilberforce, Clarkson also devoted his entire life to the ending of slavery because truth demanded that he take such a position, despite the popular support for slavery in eighteenth-century Great Britain. He believed that truth so entirely that he remained committed despite opposition and a thousand distractions, and it worked. While Wilberforce famously spoke in front of Parliament, it was Clarkson who rode from town to town across England collecting information that was compiled in a pamphlet titled "A Summary View of the Slave Trade and of the Probable Consequences of its Abolition." This little pamphlet played a significant part in the turning of public opinion in favor of abolition. It took twenty years for a bill abolishing slavery to be passed, but it would never have happened had Clarkson not believed so entirely that this was something worth doing.[2]

Because Thomas Clarkson believed that human dignity was a matter of truth, he was inspired to invest his entire life in the war to end slavery despite the fact that he didn't receive the notoriety he deserved. Truth demanded his commitment whether or not anyone knew about it and whether or not he received any credit.

If you believe something is true, but you're not willing to fight for it, your actions are saying you do not really believe it. Faith, with truth at its heart, *demands* commitment.

OUR WORK CALLS US TO COMMITMENT

———

Within the modern church, there is a subconscious bias against choosing a career that is not "for the kingdom." For some reason we think that unless we are pastors, missionaries, or evangelists, our work doesn't really matter to God.

But what if we don't want to be in ministry? What if we don't feel passionate about living in a developing country, wrangling with the strife a pastor has to deal with, or accosting strangers with the gospel?

The idea that the only valid career for a Christian is one in the ministry is simply not true. Christianity does not teach that "secular" work is any less holy than "sacred" work. The Bible does not advocate a position that gives pre-eminence to those who work in the ministry as opposed to those who work in the marketplace, and actually, some of Christianity's greatest contributions to world history haven't come from her pulpits but from her entrepreneurs, her educators, her doctors, and her political leaders.

Florence Nightingale is a wonderful example. Born in Italy on May 12, 1820, the daughter of a well-to-do English family, Florence was raised to be a debutante. However, she was uncomfortable in social situations and her social-climbing, ambitious mother despaired of her awkwardness. The mother and daughter often clashed over Mrs. Nightingale's plans for Florence's future.

Florence was highly educated by her father and was taught religion, philosophy, and modern languages, and at age sixteen experienced what she later referred to as a calling from God, urging her to go out and work for him. She was unsure what that work was to be, but soon began to feel that nursing offered her the best way to serve God and limit human suffering.

Her mother, naturally, was horrified; no well-bred English girl at that time would have been allowed to train to be something as plebeian as a nurse. She was expected to marry a well-to-do man and be a wife and mother. It took some time for Florence to convince her parents, but they finally consented to allow her to attend nursing training in Kaiserwerth, Germany.[3] Her training complete, Florence became the administrator for a hospital in London, and when the Crimean War began in 1853, Florence received a letter from the British government asking her to lead a team of trained nurses to care for the wounded soldiers in Turkey.[4] When they arrived they found the hospitals filthy, the mortality rates high due more to disease than injury, supplies inadequate, and even the doctors unwilling to enter the wards for fear of catching disease themselves.

But Florence was unshaken. She ordered supplies, enlisted soldiers' wives to help with their care, and insisted that every soldier receive clean clothing, baths, and fresh bedding. Though Florence and her nurses were forbidden from entering the wards at night because it was considered improper, she still made rounds throughout the night carrying a lantern, which earned her the nickname "The Lady with the Lamp" among the soldiers. Because of their commitment to their calling and care for their patients, Florence and her team reduced the mortality rate in the hospital at Scutari from 33 percent to 2 percent in only a few months, notwithstanding the contempt of the doctors and the inefficiency of the British government.[5]

Once the Crimean War ended, Florence returned to England. Despite suffering chronic pain from contracting a bacterial infection in Turkey, which would keep her periodically confined to her bed for the rest of her life, she began at once to work on reforming the training of nurses and the conditions of military and public hospitals.[6] She even met Queen Victoria and Prince Albert to discuss hospital reform. And when her illness became so severe that she could not leave her room, she wrote hundreds of letters to politicians, hospital administrators, and fellow nurses, urging for better conditions for patients in British hospitals and better training for nurses.

Today Florence Nightingale is considered the founder of modern nursing, and her reforms have revolutionized medicine all over the world. Florence's testimony is the story of a woman who viewed her work as her calling, and from that calling she channeled the commitment required to live her entire life against expectations. And thank God, she did. The world is a different and better place because of it.

Christians have always believed that our work, sacred or secular, is not simply a job to be completed, but a calling to be enjoyed. When you think of work this way, it changes the way you view everything you do from nine to five, and commitment comes along more easily. When everything you do at work may be the thing that changes someone else's life, your daily grind at the office turns into an adventure to rival the dream career you wanted as a child.

OUR RELATIONSHIPS NEED OUR COMMITMENT

There is no such thing as relationship without commitment—it simply doesn't exist. Whether in its most shallow form or in its most tenacious, commitment is the glue that holds a relationship together. Our culture popularly disagrees with this idea, and it does so to its detriment. These days it's more common to believe that "love," some sort of feeling or inclination, is the foundation for a strong relationship, but the *love* of the Bible isn't a feeling at all. It's a choice—a choice to commit to one another, whether or not that commitment is supported by feelings.

It's like the story of Kim and Krickitt Carpenter.

After being married for just two months, they were on their way to a family member's house for Thanksgiving when they were hit by another car. Their accident was horrific, and it left Krickitt, only twenty-four years old, in a coma for four months. When she emerged from the coma, she had completely lost any memory of the last two years. Her entire relationship with her husband, Kim, had vanished from her mind, and she lost the ability to do even simple tasks.

Kim remained committed to Krickitt, even though she didn't remember him. He had made a vow to love her until the end and he stayed with her. Through months of therapy, Kim did all he could to try and get Krickitt to fall in love with him again. Eventually they restarted their relationship from the beginning and were married again three years later. Their amazing love story inspired the hit motion picture *The Vow*, and Kim has been quick to tell the world that it was their relationship with God that inspired their commitment to one another and that their story is meant to "illuminate God's hand in it all."[7]

We live our lives in relationships with imperfect people. We hurt each other, we make mistakes, and we give each other plenty of reasons to run away. If our relationships don't have commitment to hold them together, they simply will not survive the pressures and imperfections of life. C. S. Lewis wrote, "Love is not an affectionate feeling, but a steady wish for the loved person's ultimate good as far as it can be obtained."[8] In other words, we must be committed to the temporal and eternal well-being of those with whom we have relationships, whether it's our spouses, our children, or our friends.

OUR CHARACTER IS FORGED THROUGH COMMITMENT

So much of what makes one a person of integrity, a person whose character is trustworthy, is forged in the crucible of commitment. You become a person of patience when your commitment requires you to stick with something when it is challenging. You become a person freed by contentment when your commitments require that you live with what you have, where you are. You become a person who is trustworthy when you do what's right over what's easy or expedient, because your commitment to faith demands that you do so.

One such person was Cornelia "Corrie" ten Boom, who was born April 14, 1892, in what is now the Netherlands. She and her large family lived in an old house above a watch shop that she and her father ran together. When the Nazis occupied Holland in 1940, Corrie and her family began to take in Jewish refugees, hiding them in their home, in a secret compartment they built to shelter their guests during raids. In doing so, the family helped as many as eight hundred Jews escape the Nazis.[9]

However, a Dutch informant reported their activities to the Gestapo, and Corrie and all her family were arrested and sent to Sheveningen prison, where Corrie's father, Casper, who was then eighty-four, died ten days after being imprisoned. After four months in prison, Corrie and her sister Betsie were transferred to the Vught political concentration camp, where they were held for another three months before moving to the Ravensbrueck death camp.[10] Betsie died in the camp in December of that year, only weeks before Corrie was suddenly released. Corrie later learned that her release was a clerical error; she had actually been slated for execution.

In her biography *The Hiding Place*, ten Boom wrote about her time in the camp as one of utter horror but of the constant awareness of God's love: "There is no pit so deep that He is not deeper."[11] After the war Corrie traveled the world, speaking about her experience and about the love of God that carried her through it. She opened rehabilitation centers in her native country to minister to Jewish Holocaust survivors, as well as the Dutch displaced by the war.[12] She was honored as Righteous Among the Nations by the nation of Israel in 1967.[13]

To this day Corrie ten Boom is spoken of as one of history's greatest heroes because she rose to the occasion when history came calling. The only reason why she had the strength to do so was because of the character built within her and her family, before God needed them to help save so many lives. People like Corrie were so committed to the belief that every person is made in the image of God that they had the character to risk their very lives to do what was right. Imagine how many millions of lives throughout history would have met tragedy without men and women whose integrity demanded that they act when others remained silent? Their integrity and commitment were so strong that they were able to rise to the occasion when their moment came to make history.

We all hope a person of integrity would be willing to stand up for us in our time of need. Why, then, is it that we fail to embrace for ourselves the strength we admire so greatly in others?

ELEVEN

STARING DOWN THE OPPOSITION

What's holding me back
from commitment?

PAUL ONCE WROTE, "WHOEVER KNOWS THE RIGHT thing to do and fails to do it, for him it is sin" (James 4:17 ESV). We've all felt that feeling. We've fussed at ourselves in the mirror for not doing something we should've done.

At the root of these "sins of omission" (as theologians call them), we almost always find commitment issues. We leave things undone that should have been done because we couldn't follow through at the moment. Despite the fact that we know what we should have done and that we tell ourselves that it would have been better had we done it, we still have trouble following through.

Why? We can all agree on the benefits of commitment—we've seen that people motivated by commitment do great things, and we've seen how God uses committed people for his glory. But if commitment is so clearly important, then why is it so hard for us? Why do we struggle to finish our projects, maintain our relationships, and build our faith? Why is it so hard even when we know how great the benefits are?

There are a lot of reasons for this, and in order to move past them, we need to know what they are and understand some of the major reasons.

WE LIVE IN A PESSIMISTIC CULTURE

Could it be that we struggle with commitment so fiercely because everyone around us seems to be struggling with it as well? We see our friends and family members slacking in their faith, giving up on their relationships, and abandoning their dedication to their jobs, and we assume that the ability to commit simply isn't that important anymore, or that we're not capable of doing it. We feel the pain of divorce in our families, we see the consequences of halfhearted faith, and despite knowing the painful consequences of our failures, we still struggle with commitment.

Eventually we begin thinking pessimistically about it

all, and we expect our own stories to end like everyone else's. We think that, despite our best efforts, we, too, will become a casualty on the side of some road, somewhere. That we'll relapse or cheat or just end up living an apathetic life. And—if we're not careful—we'll become our own self-fulfilling prophecy.

If we don't learn to think positively and optimistically about our ability to follow through on our commitments, then we simply will not do it because we will play out our lives according to the script constructed in our minds. We will move in the direction that we tell ourselves we're most likely to go. This is why it is so desperately important to keep positive and believe that we are all capable of commitment.

OUR CULTURE CONDITIONS US TO FIGHT COMMITMENT

We are immersed in a culture that demands everything instantly, and it has conditioned in us a lack of patience. We find it difficult to maintain the simplest of commitments, especially when the commitment becomes challenging. We're not able to persevere the way people once did because our tolerance for adversity has declined so dramatically in our fast-paced and pampered culture.

High-speed Internet, fast food, and instant updates on social media have taught us to expect that we can have anything we want at the drop of a hat without having to wait or work for it. The idea that we have to put in effort and wait for a return is almost offensive to those of us who've been sucked hopelessly into this world that tolerates nothing less than instant gratification. We feel nostalgic for a time when people talked face to face and meals were homemade, yet that nostalgia doesn't seem to stop us from texting at the table during dinner.

Just for a change, try putting away the smartphone the next time you're out for coffee with a friend. You may be surprised how much you enjoy the break, and also how difficult it is to stay 100 percent committed to the conversation you're having with the person sitting across the table from you.

WE FEEL ENTITLED

Commitment is also hard for us because we have a prevailing sense of entitlement that convinces us that everyone else should do the hard work for us. Entitlement is the enemy of commitment because it deceives us into thinking that others are responsible for our success— our bosses ought to incentivize our achievements, our spouses ought to treat us a certain way, and our society ought to make it easier for us to get a break. When we believe that we deserve something merely on the basis of our own merits, we fail to look realistically at our own weaknesses, and we find ourselves struggling to work hard in order to stay committed because we think everything should be handed to us.

Our society fuels this sense of entitlement that stunts our maturity, hamstrings our ambition, and destroys our sense of reality. We will only maintain our commitments by reminding ourselves that nothing in life is guaranteed to us. While God promises us that all things work together for our good, nowhere in the Bible are Christians given a pass. On the contrary, we have a responsibility to count ourselves less than others, to know our own weaknesses, and to make sure that we praise him for every blessing he has given us, even when we think we have done something great ourselves.

There's so much thinking in our society today that gives us permission to be lazy and shift responsibility from us to others or to God. If we could stop feeling as if God owes us an explanation and as if people ought to give us a break, we might have the gusto to move forward in our lives with a realistic sense of what it'll take to accomplish our goals. Commitment would seem less like an inconvenience and more like a responsibility.

WE DON'T COUNT THE COST

Commitment is not cheap. It's not easy, and you're not going to get to the finish line unless it costs you something. No one stays committed by accident.

It reminds me of the story of the eccentric millionaire Charles Bedaux, who funded and led an expedition to Northern British Columbia in 1934. The expedition was intended to serve as a publicity stunt, as well as a public test of the Citroën half-track cars being developed by Bedaux's friend André Citroën. However, Bedaux had absolutely no experience leading any kind of expedition, and from the very beginning, the trip was a disaster—the packing list included luxury items such as champagne, truffles, silk pajamas, and fine china, none of which would really be of any use in the Canadian north.

The expedition was comprised of more than a hundred people, including Hollywood film director Frank Crosby, who would later be known for his work on the film *High Noon*, and Bedaux's Italian mistress as well as his wife. The intended route covered fifteen hundred miles, much of it over uncharted terrain. The group set off on July 6 from Edmonton, Alberta. Plagued by terrible weather conditions, the faulty construction of their vehicles, and the death of many of their horses from disease, Bedaux eventually realized that they had to turn back. But rather than blame their failure on his own poor leadership, he decided to fabricate a catastrophe. The Citroen half-tracks had proven poorly adapted to the terrain and needed to be disposed of, so Bedaux had them pushed off a cliff, then reported to the newspapers that they had been lost in a freak accident, which necessitated the group's return.[1] Yet, the truth was Bedaux's failure wasn't thrust upon him by circumstance—it was invited by his lack of foresight and preparation.

When we accept Jesus' salvation, we embark on a journey. Conversion isn't the end of faith's journey—it is just the beginning. Theologians speak of salvation as a point in time, but also as a process of sanctification. And, like any adventure, there will be some difficulties and challenges along the way, and you must be prepared for these at the onset of the journey.

What will happen when our commitment to God's will meets the gritty reality of a secular world that neither knows nor cares about our devotion to God? We might find ourselves battered and bruised, our egos crushed, and our plans discouraged. And when that happens, we have a decision to make. We can stand firm because we are committed, or we can flinch in the face of adversity.

The only way you'll actually stand firm is if you have adequately prepared yourself for the inevitable opposition. Otherwise, you'll be caught scrambling for answers in the eye of the storm.

Don't expect the world you're living in to give you a

break. It is governed by a different value system, and it's high time we start taking responsibility for our own lives and stop expecting others to do the heavy lifting for us. If you believe that commitment is a virtue worth having, then do something about it, and do what it takes so you won't waver when trials come your way.

TWELVE

FIVE STEPS AND A BIG TREE

How can I become more committed?

I HAVE A FRIEND WHO LIKES TO RANT—AND I DON'T mean "complain." I mean "rant" as exercising some major league, out-of-control, very serious angst in the most voluble form. Most of the time I disagree with him, but this time I didn't: "I wish these preachers actually understood life. I'm so tired of hearing them stand in their pulpits and go on and on about how I should live my life, what I should avoid, and what I should do and shouldn't do. And the entire time, I'm thinking, *if this guy actually had any clue whatsoever what it was like to live in the real world, then maybe more people would come to this church.* I think that half the preachers in the world ought to talk less, listen more, and when they try and tell us how to live our lives they ought to at least be practical about it.

I agree with my friend because I, too, think far too many spiritual leaders have their noses so deeply in books and so far away from everyday life that they don't have the ability to teach the Bible in a way that seems relevant to the average person sitting in the pew trying to make sense of this crazy world. This became especially apparent to me several years ago when I became a vice president at Liberty University and was tasked with an enormous amount of "secular" responsibilities. I essentially became a tentmaker who preached on the weekends, an executive Monday through Friday. It was the best possible thing that could have happened to my ministry, because I was suddenly ejected out of the unusual world of full-time ministry into the rigors of the nine-to-five.

My new job gave me a new perspective, and at the cost of being a hypocrite, I'm going to provide you with some practical information I've discovered that can help you strengthen your commitments. I suggest that you enter into a season of focusing on this part of your life and attempt to apply each of these five steps. The season can be as long or as short as you'd like—a week, a semester, or a year. It may take longer for some than for others, depending on where you are in life and how hard you are willing to work on it. Regardless, it's helpful to have a period of time devoted to focusing on these steps.

1: CONSIDER YOUR FOUNDATION

While your ability to commit isn't a matter of your personality, it *is* a matter of your identity. It's based upon what you believe about the world on a fundamental level. In a previous book called *Honestly*, I spent a lot of time on this issue. I attempted to answer the question, "Why do we struggle to live what we say we believe?"

Most Christians I know struggle with living out what they *know* is true in their hearts. But the struggle is not a matter of knowing whether something is true or not; it's a matter of whether they are going to live out that truth. It's a matter of reminding themselves of what they know is true and trying to apply it to their everyday lives. There are lots of things that we know to be true as Christians, but there are some things that are at the bottom of the pyramid, the foundational ideas upon which everything else in our lives is built. These include ideas like the deity and resurrection of Christ, the inerrancy of the Word of God, the primacy of the gospel, and the reality of sin. Ask yourself whether you believe them to be true, and then look very carefully at your normal life and ask yourself to what degree these truths are influencing the decisions you make, the way you're living, your plans for your future, and how you interact with others.

Do your relationships with your coworkers and friends reflect the fact that you know they bear the image of God? Do you plan for your future with the knowledge that a sovereign God charts your steps? When you fail, do you seek forgiveness from your resurrected Savior and move on in the awareness that his blood covers you and removes your shame forever? This exercise will help you understand how large a gap exists between what you know is true and how you live your daily life.

Once you've reflected on this, work on each of the weak points. Memorize Scripture, challenge yourself to live a little different for just one day, and ask for the help of others. Embrace this step as you would any other. It's like a kid who gets interested in baseball—he learns the rules and then he starts to apply them in practice and then in games, and then he's a baseball player. The same thing is true of your faith. Learn about it, practice it, and eventually you'll become it.

2: CHOOSE VERY FEW THINGS AS THE OBJECTS OF YOUR COMMITMENT

While the first point speaks mainly to the theological implications of commitment, commitment is one of those aspects of life that has profound implications on both a transcendent and practical level. One thing you quickly discover about the practice of commitment is that it is demanding. You can't commit to everything. You have to commit to the most important things every day. This means that you have to learn how to prioritize and decide what is most important. Try to do this every night before you go to bed or when you first wake up in the morning. Turn off your phone, go outside, or sit down in your favorite chair, and think about what deserves and needs your attention today and filter those obligations through the commitments that demand your highest priority.

Our main obligations can usually be placed into three categories: our faith, our families, and our work, in that order. Our faith comes first because it is the spring from which our other commitments find their source. Our family comes next because God has connected us with these particular people for a reason and we should love them more than anyone else—or anything else—on this planet, and our responsibilities to them should be our foremost priority, not only because God commanded it, but because the family is the foundation of all of society, and healthy families mean healthy communities, which we as Christians are tasked with creating. Finally, our work: we have discussed before that our jobs are not merely means to pay our bills, but are our callings, the

things to which we are to devote our energy and advance
God's kingdom in whatever capacity—sacred or secular—
he designed us for.

All of us have a thousand things vying for our attention every single day. You will never have time to do all
you need to do on any given day. It's not even worth trying. You must decide what's best, what's most worthy of
your time, and never let your values be subservient to the
chaos around you.

3: SET SOME GOALS

It's much easier to stay committed when you have goals,
whether they are short term or long term. Even if those
goals are arbitrary, there's something about knowing
where you're going that allows you the strength to press
on when it gets difficult. It also gives you a way of mea-
suring success, to take those rare moments of quiet and
contemplation and think about how far you've come and
how far you have yet to go.

Not too long ago I made the decision to live a health-
ier lifestyle. I decided to eat better and lose some weight.
I hired a brutal trainer who nearly killed me twice a week,
but when he said, "There's just three more reps to go,"
I found out that I was stronger than I thought. Even if
a moment before I felt as if I couldn't do one more rep,

I was able to do three more knowing that I was getting closer to the finish line. You only know how strong you are when you press your limits.

Life is like taking a hike to the summit of a mountain. It's easier to get there when you know that each forward step is one step closer. We have a tendency to go through life randomly, to just work for the sake of working, and we feel as if we're on one of those hamster wheels, rolling around and around without going anywhere. This isn't helpful, and no one that does something great with his or her life has this mentality. Direction is essential to commitment; working blindly will never allow us to accomplish the goals that we have set. Even Jesus himself admonished us to keep the end goal in mind, and the author of the book of Hebrews advises us to keep our eyes on the finish line (Heb. 12:1–3). God does this because he knows how we're made. He knows that we need direction to give our lives purpose, to move forward motivated by the awareness of our goals.

4: PUT IT ALL ON PAPER

Here's a well-known but ill-applied fact: even if something's important, you're going to forget it unless you write it down. As you go through this exercise in evaluating your commitments, write down as much of what you're thinking as possible. Mark Driscoll put it best: "When we write down what we learn, we are forced to sharpen our understanding."[1] I've found this to be true in my own experience. As I write, I channel greater creativity and clarity. There's something happening between my mind and my hands that helps me better understand what I'm actually thinking and feeling.

Many times I'm amazed at what comes up when I sit down to write. As the words form, I understand whatever it is I'm writing about with greater precision. The famous twentieth-century writer Flannery O'Connor once said, "I write because I don't know what I think until I read what I say."[2] This is what happens when we process things on paper; it gives us the chance to evaluate our own thoughts in a way that the abstract process of thinking simply can't do.

So go through this exercise with a pen in hand, and not only will you have a greater sense of where exactly your struggles are and what you must do to combat them, you will also have in pen-and-ink a chronicle of the change you have experienced.

5: GET A FEW CLOSE CONFIDANTS

Finally, never forget that Christianity is meant to be lived out in community. A lonely person cannot be a healthy person, and individuals are not meant to bear life's greatest challenges on their own. All of us have experienced the need to find a friend and ask advice, share struggles, or just plain vent to them about the frustrations of our day. Doing so brings not only relief but the strength to push forward toward our goals, knowing that someone else understands and supports you.

Choose your confidants carefully. Do you have older and wiser people in your life whom you can speak to as you're making big decisions and trying to navigate life's hurdles? Is there someone of a similar age or situation you can talk to about the struggles you share and how you overcome them? And is there someone younger than you or in a stage of life you've already experienced who can benefit from what you've learned? When we are in community with others, we discover that even the things with which we struggle are not so different; God sometimes sends us down the same hard roads so we can guide the ones who come after. Jesus once said that his disciples would be known by their love for one another (John 13:35). One of the ways we demonstrate that love is by supporting one another in our struggles.

There are a few people, some in my hometown and some farther away, to whom I go when I'm trying to make a major decision. I just track them down when I need to talk. If it's a huge decision, then I'll even travel out of town to meet with them rather than simply speaking with them over the phone. I can honestly say that I haven't made a single major decision in my life without consulting these people. They're my personal board of advisors. They are very wise and care deeply about me, as I do about them. When we talk about one another's lives, there is a sense of "we're in this together." That's the mark of strong community, and that's the secret to not roaming through life aimlessly. Have these people in your life, and bring them into your pursuit of greater commitment. Take their advice and invite them to ask you the difficult questions and assess your progress. The accountability this brings into your relationships is a helpful, and even necessary, part of maintaining your commitments.

My friend Rick Warren is fond of a particular sermon illustration he draws from his childhood. He sometimes speaks of the gigantic redwood trees of northern California, emphasizing the fact that these massive objects—the largest and oldest living things on earth—do not have deep roots. Their roots are actually quite shallow for their enormous height, but they are intertwined with other redwoods, and that's how they remain stable for centuries despite wind and rain, earthquakes, fires, and other natural calamities. Their strength isn't in how deep their roots go, but in how intertwined their roots are with others. The same is true of our lives, and the same is true of this step. Commitment is fostered in the green house of God's community.

IT'S WORTH IT

———

This will not be an easy journey, but it will make all the difference in your life. Time and again, history tells the tales of men and women whose success hinged not on their natural or special gifts, even when those were considerable, but on how committed they were to a dream even when they seemed to be an island on their own.

The single greatest contributing factor to personal success is your ability to follow through on your commitments, and it is what it will take for you to stick to God's will once you find it. The world is busting at the seams with people whose fantastic ideas would make it a better place if they were just committed enough to follow through on those dreams. Sometimes it's the little things that kill us, but this one is not little. It's everything, and it's entirely in our power to make a change for the better, to turn ourselves into the kind of die-hard, committed people whose drive to follow the will of God will repair our shattered world.

It's like one of my mentors once told me: "You don't measure success by a man's talent or wealth, as the world does, but rather by what it takes to discourage him." If something is important—and your faith is important—it's worth sticking to, even if all of hell opposes you.

PART 3

HOW WOULD THE WORLD LOOK IF CHRISTIANS FOLLOWED GOD'S WILL?

THIRTEEN

THE GROCERY DANCE

Learning to dream again

WHEN WE LIVE IN CONFUSION ABOUT GOD'S WILL FOR our lives, we end up losing the ability to live life to its fullest. We give up on our dreaming and revert to mediocrity. Yet that isn't how God designed us. He designed us with ambition ingrained into our beings. I've never met someone without ambition, and neither have you. Why? Because there's something innately human about dreaming and hoping for a brighter future.

It's evident in every child who wants to fly away to distant planets and become an adventurer. It's the theme of every fairy tale; the hero or heroine who becomes something new and better before the "happily ever after" closes the scene. And examples are never too far away—just ask some children what they want to be when they grow up. They will answer in outlandish ways—they want to be astronauts and scientists, fire fighters and doctors—as if these things can be accomplished only by wishing. While they're at it, they want to scale the highest peaks, conquer the Sahara desert, and invent wings that allow a man to fly.

Kids don't see the natural limits that hem us in and bind us up. They live in a world where miracles are just a part of the everyday and where the whole world looks like one fantastic and mythical play. For children, the sky really is the limit. It's almost as if it has been scripted in our DNA to dream big dreams—and believe that they can come true. It's as though God gives children a blank slate so they can draw upon it anything they dare to dream. And they do. Ask a child about his or her dreams and listen to the answers you get. It is a glimpse into the beauty of the blank slate, and we adults say, "Yes! You can do anything you put your mind to." And there was a time, maybe so long ago we have almost forgotten, when we believed it.

DREAMING AGAIN

Consider Carol. She used to dream about God's purpose for her life, but now her life is basically summed up in the sweat trickling down her forehead when she arrives home from work, lugging fourteen bags of groceries with her two kids in tow.

It's hard to open the front door holding fourteen bags of groceries. It's like an Olympic sport in the world of home economics. She leans to the side and lifts her right hip just enough that her pinky finger can loop itself around the key in her pocket. The whole time she's cursing herself, wondering why she refuses to make multiple trips to and from the car with the groceries.

She twists her whole frame, freeing the key chain, and gets the key in position. Success! Then the dog barks, and scares the kids. Which scares her. Which causes her to drop the key. Which makes the dog bark louder. The kids scream. She leans down to get the key. She knocks her head on the doorknob—instant headache. She reaches for her head, and a rogue apple drops out of a grocery bag and rolls across the floor. The dog runs off with the apple. The kids start laughing shrilly, loudly. Carol thinks the kids are laughing at her. Like the dog, she barks at them, only to apologize when she realizes she was wrong, again.

Everyone tumbles wildly into the house. The kids and the dog run past Carol. They are a mess. She is a mess. The whole world is a mess. Her business suit is as tired and wrinkled as she is and her hair looks like she just came down from one of those tornadoes that destroy trailer parks in the Midwest. Her mom would have called her "frazzled," and that would have been a good description. Her mom never looked frazzled for some reason, but it was her favorite way of describing Carol.

Frazzled. It's a colorful word that sounds the way she feels. *Frazzled.* The double Zs buzzing against her tongue like the current of panic always buzzing around her skull. Her whole life feels a bit this way these days. Her job, her family life, her schedule, her church obligations, everything . . . just plain *frazzled.* Chaos. But when it comes time for her women's small group every Saturday morning, you would think she was living the American dream. Someone in the group asks about the image that comes to mind when she thinks about her life.

"Honestly," she says—in my experience, someone saying "honestly" is the first clue that they are about to tell a lie, and she was—"my life feels like a garden. It's filled with all kinds of colorful and different things that together make up one beautiful space."

A nice, poetic reply, and a total lie. She looks around to see all the other women nodding their heads in approval. She passed the test of the question and maintained the expected façade of a perfect life. The image that actually came to her mind wasn't a garden, however—it was a train crash. The kind of crash where miles and miles of boxcars suddenly go barreling into one another at a hundred miles an hour and all you see in the pictures on the news is charred and twisted metal.

She wrestles with her dreams of the ideal life and the life she is actually living. They don't match up. Then she asks herself the same question we've all asked ourselves a time or two: *How on earth did I get here?*

ALL OF US ARE DISCONTENT—SOME OF THE TIME

Chances are, most of us have asked ourselves the question: *How did I get here?* It's part of the human experience. Life, as the old saying says of hell, is often "paved with good intentions." Maybe a better way to say it is that life is piled over with crumbled dreams.

It's like the guy I heard about the other day, whose life ambition was to own his own fishing business. He always dreamed of sailing out in the early morning sun to do what he loved best, and to earn his living by it. This was his dream. So he decided to leave his job and take on an apprenticeship with a professional fisherman, and to this day—after more than a decade—he labors, day in and day out, assisting someone else who is living out *his* dream. He's given up on the idea of owning his own business. He's decided his dream was a little too much, and now he plans on settling for a diminished version of his once-noble dream. How many people do you know with stories like this?

Nearly every adult I know began with a Plan A. Now they are on Plan C or Plan Z. They're just getting by, having long abandoned their best dream for life. Sometimes they feel that rumbling of discontent inside. Sometimes that dream peeks back at them around the corner, but now they don't have the energy to go running after it. They've cut their losses and moved on to "more reasonable" ambitions for their life.

Their—our—dreams once looked so real, didn't they?

Almost as if you could grasp them between your ten fingers and pull them close. Now they seem to float away like smoke rising from a crackling campfire. Dreams seem tantalizingly real, achievable, and just around the next bend. Then you arrive at the bend and you discover that the magnificent oasis you were waiting for was actually a mirage. What was once so real you could taste it, is now so elusive you can barely remember it.

This is why lots of people just give up dreaming all together. The whimsy of their dream crashes head on with the obligations of day-to-day life. And they give up.

IS THIS THE WAY IT'S SUPPOSED TO BE?

Life has a way of beating the dreamer out of us, and it's not kind about it either. It drains us of our enthusiasm and leaves us with barely enough energy to do what we must to survive. Life is brutal and unpredictable. It sure doesn't seem like a dream laboratory for us most of the time. It's more like a dream monster, gobbling up all the passing optimism and opportunities.

As a result, instead of thriving, most of us, much of the time, feel more as if we're just getting through. You ask yourself, *is it supposed to be this way?* Eventually you decide it is, and so you just try to get used to it. You walk along from one day to the next, one crisis to another. The good days are rare. Most days consist of just running through the motions. The grueling daily duties piling upon one another weighing you down.

We have to make one more sales call, have another half dozen meetings at the office. We cook the same meals on the same days every week, and we feel as if we're always in a hurry. Our phones are constantly buzzing to let us know where we have to be in the next thirty minutes. Life hits some kind of rhythm, which makes it predictable, at least, but at the same time it cements our feet to the floor in the malaise of the routine.

Occasionally we get tired of it all. Living isn't as easy as our parents made it seem. We find ourselves overwhelmed and frustrated. Then that dreaded state arrives: discontentedness. Everyone I know has these feelings sometimes. (In fact, discontentedness might be the reason you picked up this book in the first place.) They feel unhappy with who they are and where they are in their lives. They feel unhappy about missed opportunities and unrealized dreams. And then they feel guilty because they are "discontent." They start asking that familiar question: "What am I supposed to do with my life?" Then come the questions about God's will. Then comes the vicious cycle again.

I believe these feelings of discontent are not bad—they are good! I believe they are a gift of God and the secret to dreaming again.

FOURTEEN

WHAT'S HOLY ABOUT NOT LIKING LIFE?

*How your dissatisfaction with
life is good, not bad*

IF YOU'D LIKE TO LEARN HOW TO LIVE PERPETUALLY IN the euphoria of your dreams, then find yourself an inventor. They are the ultimate dreamers, and they hold within their peculiar tribe the two secrets to dreaming so fully that your dreams become reality. Inventors take blank slates, unlikely situations, and impossible problems, and they make them their playground. They run around in those challenges every which way, twisting and turning them in their minds, subjecting those problems to experimentation of every kind. Eventually they harness those problems and ride them to victory.

As far as inventors go, there is none more famous than

Thomas Edison. Most people would gladly settle for one great success in life, but Edison wasn't like most people. He felt a compelling need to invent for the sake of invention. He was the type of person who didn't get his joy from solving one great problem—he relished the sheer quantity of his contributions. He would challenge himself for the pleasure of it, and wrestle with a problem until it finally relented, even if it cost him nearly everything. He simply couldn't lose. No one lived a life more immersed in invention, in dreaming, than Edison.

But what was the secret to Edison's drive, and could that secret unfold for us the formula to resuscitate our latent dreaming? I believe it can, and fortunately for us, he left us clues in his own journals.

EMBRACING DISCONTENT

In his journal Edison wrote, "Discontent is the first necessity of progress."[1]

Edison—the most iconic figure in the history of American invention—knew a little something about progress. He shaped the modern world with his ideas and his experimentation, and it was from the ripe ground of discontent that he found the impetus and power to do so.

But we've been taught quite the opposite, haven't we? We've been taught to believe that when we felt a gnawing dissatisfaction with our lives that we ought to ignore it, to push it deep down where it can't hurt us anymore. We ought to flee from it, we're told. Discontentedness is a vice, not a virtue, after all.

But being discontent didn't force Edison to live an unsatisfied life fraught with second thoughts about what might have been had he made different choices in the past. His discontentedness didn't cause him to complain ad nauseam about the problems in his life and in the world. Instead Edison cultivated discontent as a powerful agent to motivate him to invent again. His attitude toward this potentially harmful emotion redeemed it, and allowed it to be turned into good.

On a very fundamental level, he attempted to change what he didn't like about the world he was living in precisely *because* he wasn't satisfied with it. Being discontent turned out to be the catalyst for change in his life. It's what caused him to ask himself what could be different in the world, and to dare to make that difference reality. It gave him the motivation to test things and fail—many times—but eventually to succeed, and one success on one great experiment had the power to make a thousand failures seem less significant.

He listened to his discontent and then reacted to it in a positive way. It was from his discontented place that he drudged up the ability to invent, and to invent again. Discontentedness drove him to the shop day after day.

He wouldn't settle for the way things were. He always imagined how they might be, how they could be if someone—if he—tried to do something about it.

This part of the secret to Edison's success doesn't need much explanation. Discontent is a common experience for most of us. Everyone feels it sometimes. Discontent can, if allowed to run amuck, make a mess of our lives, but if we control it and we use it—if we think differently about it—then it can become a powerful motivation for us to dream again and to turn those dreams into reality.

In God's great scheme of things, it's discontentedness that reminds us to dream again, to go after God's will again, to dig down deep and stay committed for the long haul. It's discontentedness that promotes the possibility of change, and it's discontentedness that rouses us from the ease of the everyday.

Ask yourself this holy question: What makes you feel discontent?

PRESSING ON

It wasn't simply Edison's angst with the status quo that made him a person of such historical consequence. Discontent might have the power to rouse change, but it doesn't have the ability to actually make change on its own.

Edison's second—and more important—secret to

success is easy enough to understand, but is much more difficult to live. There's nothing natural about it. Yet it's so necessary. The second secret to Edison's success was his unrelenting devotion to whatever dream arrested him in the moment. Once he set his mind upon a goal, there was almost nothing that could derail him from it. He grabbed on to it until his knuckles turned white, and you would have to pry it out of his dying hands before he would release it.

Edison, at the core of who he was, must have believed that almost anything was possible if you were sufficiently focused upon it. He famously said that "genius is 1 percent inspiration and 99 percent perspiration."[2] That wasn't just some trite phrase he rolled off of his lips during a motivational speech—it was his daily habit.

You see it most clearly in Edison's positive attitude about failure. He once said, "I have not failed. I've just found ten thousand ways that won't work."[3] Failure didn't represent the end of the road; it was a mile marker on his way to success. If the greatest people in history were brought together, they would all have at least one thing in common: they were built by failure. Edison was ferocious in his commitment to progress, and his tenacity caused him to try again and again after every failure (and there were plenty of them), knowing that around the next bend might rest the solution he had been looking for.

What a shame it would be, he must have said to

himself a thousand times, *if I were one more experiment away from solving this problem?* He believed discontent was a necessity of progress, but it wasn't enough to just feel frustration with the way things were—he had to do something about it, knowing that whatever that "something" was might take many hours, many tries, and many failures. But if it was worth it, he wouldn't let go. He would commit to the challenge at hand, and commit to the very end. And he did, over and over again. And the world is better for it.

It's no wonder that Edison patented 1,093 mechanisms and processes during his career.[4] His creations included: a stock ticker, a mechanical vote recorder, electrical power, recorded music, motion pictures, and even a battery that would operate an electric car! Some have even said that Edison alone invented the twentieth century.[5]

OUR PROBLEM

You might wonder why it is that I'm finishing this book on God's will this way. Why would I be dredging up these feelings of discontent, and compelling you to dream big dreams again?

It's because I believe the anxiety surrounding "God's will" has caused too many people to give up too early on life and to miss the opportunities they have to contribute to the world. I believe that the things in our hearts that cause us dissatisfaction might be the leftover rumblings of God's original call on our lives. I believe that God made us dreamers for a reason, and that there are too many unrealized dreams in too many lives.

So it's time to stop making excuses and start turning the dials of history that are yours to turn.

We need you.

God has given you a dream that could change the world.

It's your choice whether you will give it a whirl.

FIFTEEN

YOU ARE IMPORTANT

What disease might you cure?

You've probably never heard of Dr. Selman Waksman, yet he is one of the most important people in modern history. He slid into history almost unnoticed, but literally left the world turned up on its end.

Waksman was born in 1888 near Kiev, in modern-day Ukraine, and immigrated to the United States in 1911 to attend Rutgers College, where he earned a bachelor of science in agriculture. He later earned his PhD in biochemistry from the University of California, and then he returned to Rutgers and began to study microorganisms in the soil.[1] During the course of his research, he stumbled upon some bacteria that could produce compounds that would inhibit the growth of, or even kill, other microorganisms. This cataclysmic discovery led to an incredibly lengthy process in which he and his team of researchers placed various bacteria in petri dishes to see which of them would dominate the others. They studied scores of microorganisms, and in the process discovered a bacterium that would attack and kill *Streptococcus pneumoniae*, the organism responsible for causing certain types of pneumonia. As a result, Waksman was inspired to study other antibiotic organisms, and in 1941 he discovered a compound called actinomycin, which could both kill and slow the growth of other bacteria.[2]

Sounds good, right? Well, it wasn't. Actinomycin is toxic to all living organisms—not just other bacteria—and had little or no therapeutic application. Waksman was, naturally, disappointed. He had hoped his work would lead to an antibiotic that would assist people in fighting off disease, not kill them. A lesser person would have abandoned their efforts, discouraged and pessimistic about the prospect of future research, but not Waksman.

For another three years, Waksman pressed on. He and his assistants continued to research antibiotics, testing sample after sample and taking reams of notes. And in 1944 they finally discovered streptomycin, a broad-spectrum antibiotic that proved effective against diseases like the bubonic plague, influenza, and, most importantly, tuberculosis.[3] Tuberculosis alone had been responsible for as much as 40 percent of working-class deaths in cities in the nineteenth century.[4] All three Bronte sisters, Franz Kafka, and many others had died of this disease, in which death was virtually guaranteed since the cause of tuberculosis was unknown. Waksman's discovery was the means of saving millions of lives, and some of those lives would themselves contribute great innovations that would save others.

All of this because Dr. Waksman was willing to stick with his job even when it seemed that it was going nowhere. He didn't allow even a major setback to deter him from his commitment, and he always imagined what could happen if his life was meant to make an important contribution to history. Waksman had a type of determination and perseverance that seems especially rare these days.

Like Waksman and Edison would tell us, we never know when one more day of pressing on would have made a lifetime of difference to the world. That extra day might be *the* day when everything changes, when we step into our moment in history and take center stage. There are a thousand innovations yet to be made by those who have the courage to press on when everything seems to discourage them from doing so, and that extra day may even change history.

See, I believe that there isn't a single human being living on this planet who doesn't have a God-ordained purpose for living. I believe that every single life is of great and eternal significance, and God is constructing your story from before you were even born. If he told you the plans he has for you, you wouldn't even believe them.

A MAN WHO SAVED MILLIONS

William Booth was born April 10, 1829, in Nottingham-shire, England, and was an especially unlikely figure to make an important contribution to history. His father died when Booth was only fourteen, leaving him to help provide for the family as a pawnbroker's apprentice, a job he hated.[5] This time in his life was marked by severe poverty, and he learned to hate the suffering it caused. Later he moved to London, and in 1849 he left his pawnbroker's job in Nottingham to become a preacher in London.[6] In 1865, Booth and his wife, Catherine, founded the Christian Revival Society, which would later come to be known as the Salvation Army.[7] His organization remains hugely influential around the globe, and last year in the United States alone it served more than thirty million individuals.[8]

It all began with a single man whose heart was broken for those struggling with physical and spiritual poverty; he and his wife just began by providing food, clothing, and sanitation for the poorest of London's East End. For the rest of his life, Booth traveled all over the world, preaching the gospel and advocating for social reform. His congregation in London consisted of reformed prostitutes, gamblers, and drunks; because of this, his church was not accepted by the Church of England. But Booth and his wife weren't dissuaded from their compassion by this institutional rejection. Instead, they invested their lives all the more into their organization and developed better ways to serve the poor and spread the gospel.

Booth, whose passion for serving amounted to a military fervor, was famous for his fiery sermons, urging those who heard him to action. He once declared:

> While women weep, as they do now, I'll fight; while little children go hungry, as they do now, I'll fight; while men go to prison, in and out, in and out, as they do now, I'll fight; while there is a drunkard left, while there is a poor lost girl upon the streets, while there remains one dark soul without the light of God, I'll fight; I'll fight to the very end![9]

My favorite William Booth quote gives a glimpse into his firebrand personality: "If I thought I could win *one* more soul to the Lord by walking on my head and playing a tambourine with my toes, I'd—I'd learn how."[10]

It wasn't enough that God had a plan for Booth's life, and that Booth began immediately to live out that plan. It's that Booth's own life experience, as a poor and struggling child in an underprivileged part of his community, gave him the passion to serve the world with the intensity of a firefighter rescuing a child from a house on fire.

THERE'S MORE IN US

If Waksman is the picture of perseverance, then Booth is the picture of passion. Both qualities—perseverance and passion—are indispensible for whatever it is that you intend on doing with your life. I'm convinced that most people I've met are living life below their potential. They're coasting through the world just doing what they must when they must, and they've long lost the fire in their belly.

And it isn't hard to lose this fire. We live in a world that ticks on rhythmically with relatively few surprises. We just move blindly through it, and we're so busy with all we have to do that we just don't have the margins to do what we might have done. Yet we can make a choice every day as to how fully we will live, and we mustn't ever make the choice to surrender our dreams. Dreams evolve over time, for sure, but at the core of each of our dreams is something more transcendent, something more powerful, something that many people through history have simply referred to as a "call."

It might not be that life allows you to leave your

nation and serve refugees in the developing world, as you dreamed of in college, but remember that in God's economy the "where" isn't as important as the "who." The fact that you haven't been able to do exactly what you dreamed of doing doesn't mean that your cause is lost and your opportunity has passed. That passion, which remains dormant in your soul, need only to be resurrected and applied in the next and nearest possible way, perhaps by serving immigrants in your city or going on a missions trip during your summer vacation.

It's what Paul said to his protégé, Timothy, when he told him to "fan into flame" (2 Tim. 1:6 ESV) the gift of God that's in you. Whatever God has made you to do will be threatened by the foreboding winds of life, but don't let those embers burn out. For the love of God and for the hope of the world, keep that fire burning and do everything in your might to turn it into such a raging inferno that it consumes you entirely and forever.

We need more William Booths and Selman Waksmans, and I believe, with all my heart, that there are a few of them reading this very book, at this very point in their lives.

In fact, I think *you* might be one.

We're waiting on you to rise up and take your rightful place.

History is waiting.

SIXTEEN

THE MAP

Where to go from here

THE RICKETY MINIBUS WE WERE RIDING ON WASN'T
made for off-roading. It was rusted, creaking and cracking
in a half dozen different ways, any of which, back home,
would mean an immediate visit to a local mechanic.
I thought the entire right side was going to tumble off
when we swerved to dodge a cow that had wandered out
into the middle of the road. The old, airy windows were
no match for the thick clouds of dust that were rising up
from underneath its wheels. We were in "the-middle-of-
nowhere-India" and I wasn't sure I was going to make it
to my destination.

I've been to some pretty edgy places around the world,

but the problem is that I'm not an edgy type of person. As usual I was asking myself, *what on earth have I gotten myself into?* I had asked myself the same question when I was almost hit by a bus while trading cash on the black market in Asia (my bright idea to help some missionaries by getting a better exchange rate), when I was walking through a neighborhood known for its Islamic extremism, and when I showed up at a refugee camp in Africa two days after two aid workers had been snatched up by kidnappers and I was the only American in sight.

I have a habit of getting myself into things, with all the best intentions, of course, and this bus ride from you-know-where was no exception. Except that this time there was no chance of my dying in a fantastically adventurous way. This time, if I died, it was probably going to be from choking on a cloud of dust while riding in a rickety bus. James Bond would have never been in this situation. At one point the dust worked its way into my throat and I started coughing. It wasn't a tickle in the back of my throat—it was the hack of someone with lung cancer. My whole body was bursting from the inside, and I wondered why on earth I was subjecting myself to this awful, winding road.

See, I'm like you. I've got a really good heart until things start going really wrong. Then suddenly all my piety drains out of my pinky toe, and I start asking myself if I made a mistake. Most folks would have asked themselves that question about the time they walked up to the bus door, but not me. I had to wait until I was coughing my lungs out.

CHANGE THE PERSPECTIVE

———

Just off a serpentine side road, we found ourselves arriving at the entrance of a small village. A few dozen families had called this place home for at least a generation. It was the type of place where the random moo of a cow causes everyone's heads to turn in unison. It was compact, colorful, and strewn together.

There were rickety houses—you might call them shacks—clustered together behind crumbling, badly painted walls. Some of the houses were larger than others, but they were all home to far more people than they were meant to contain. There was the occasional pile of junk on the side of the "road," farm animals running around, and tons of kids everywhere. The kids would run up to us, posing cheek-to-cheek smiles straight into the lenses of our cameras, and they would talk to us in full sentences, as if they hadn't yet discovered that people from other places speak different languages. They must have thought we were terribly rude, or at least as dumb as rocks, as we stared wordlessly in their direction, sending them the only signal of communication we could drudge up—big, goofy smiles. They laughed, not with us, but at us.

The village was built around a massive, spreading tree, by far the largest in sight. Its huge trunk and wide canopy cast a shadow that enveloped the nearest houses like a blanket. Around its base were makeshift stools, benches, and tables. It seemed like a place where important conversations were held, where disputes were resolved. It's probably where all the local news was shared, and where some of the biggest news was made.

At the base of the tree sat half a dozen of the local old men. They were picturesque in their brightly colored turbans and long Gandalf-like beards. They sat on the same stools they must have been sitting on for decades and played games with one another. Their deck of cards looked as if it had gone through a half dozen wars, but it didn't seem to bother them a bit.

I watched for a few minutes as they played hand after hand of a card game I didn't know. They laughed continuously, jabbing one another with their jokes and teasing those who seemed a little high on their horses. At one point it almost seemed as if they were having a story-off, one-upping each other with their latest folly, or maybe they were telling the same stories again that they had told a thousand times. Each time the stories must have gotten better, because the laughter rolled upon itself like a tsunami gathering momentum. They were having pure, unadulterated fun.

Amazingly, they were having "fun" and enjoying time together without a single piece of technology tethering them to one another. They weren't sitting around a living room drinking soda and watching a big game on television. They didn't need anything but each other to enjoy life together, and they sure were enjoying it. It was the fun of a time long gone in the modern world, of sitting around a dining table having dinner every evening around the joy of knowing about everyone *else's* day, of front porch chats as folks pass by on their evening walks. It's the fun of relationships before they were confined behind digital firewalls that made it easy to keep love at arm's length, becoming vulnerable only on your own terms.

We've lost the simple way of love that lines the streets of history and was once thought of as the only joy worth finding. We've lost the ability to just be together. There were no Internet and no cell phones in that Indian village. No one was distracted by the latest television shows or social media gossip, and no one had to teach these folks what it meant to spend "quality time" with those they loved—that's all they did. They were together, going on with the rhythm of life to whatever tune it struck on that individual afternoon. They ate what little food they had, sat around open fires, talked, told stories, and sang. They gathered their greatest joy from just being together, and they welcomed me as if I was one of their own. Somehow, I felt more at home there with those strangers than I did sometimes in my own hometown.

We didn't know one another, but they knew how to live. They didn't have much, but they were committed to offering up what little they had to the best of their ability.

EMBRACE THE QUIET

Above all, that village was a quiet place. It wasn't by any means silent, but it was secluded from the mad buzzing of the world around it. It was outside the boundaries of chaos of the digital age. It wasn't filled with all kinds of worries brought upon ourselves by our need to complicate our lives with the "comforts" of the modern world. Even the ruckus around the old tree didn't disturb the quiet, because "quiet" places are different than noiseless ones.

Quiet places are those you run to when the world around you seems to be spinning frenetically on its axis. Quiet places are the oases in the desert of a life lived at the rhythm of obligation rather than at the pace of joy and peace. Quiet places are impenetrable to the myriad worries waiting on the other side of their walls. They are where you run to be who you are, and to know that no one is there to judge you.

Jesus loved quiet places. This is why, as I've written before in my book *Dirty God*, he loved the Galilee region of Israel so dearly. Its rolling hills provided a thousand corners of solace, and its hometown feel made a party out of the everyday. Jesus loved sitting on a boat on that lake, taking a nap while his friends fished, and he preferred teaching on a hillside in Galilee over a walled-in sanctuary in Jerusalem. And when he burned out—as he did—he would steal time to go for a long walk up to one of his quiet places. He'd think and pray and flee the chaos for a little bit of solace.

Like Jesus, we must flee to the quiet when the world seems to squeeze in around us, when we need to be able to think clearly and be free of its worries. Unfortunately, the quiet is elusive. In our world almost all of the quiet places have been built in and taken up, and—even more perilously—the few places that remain can be far too easily polluted. Our technology goes with us into the quiet, beeping and buzzing, always there for a quick peek, a quick reply, or a quick chat. We're not committed to the people sitting across the table from us. We're committed to the buzzing and beeping of that device helping us convince ourselves of our own importance.

It's no wonder everyone seems overwhelmed. There are a thousand things crowding out everything else, and our worlds seem in an ever-present state of turmoil. It becomes almost impossible to be firm in your commitments, much less find God's way for your life, when a thousand beeping, buzzing distractions are waiting to knock you off balance at a moment's notice.

The elusive quiet is a refuge in your time of need, a place of seclusion where you can be who you are without worrying who you're supposed to be. It's the place you go to after reading a book like this one to ask yourself, "Where do I go from here?"

GET TO IT

It was especially quiet that night when I dozed off to sleep on the roof of one of those ramshackle homes. The moon stood bright, illuminating the sky in its greyish-blue hue. Only the occasional chirp of an insect broke the silence as I went to bed with the night and arose with the morning.

It may have been the quietest place I had ever been in my life, and maybe that's why it affected me so profoundly. I visited there before I had an iPhone. I wasn't quite the technological-crack-addict then that I am now, but I still felt something off inside of me, even back then. I felt as if I was doing something wrong by not having a list of things to do when I arrived in that quiet place. Sliding into the easygoing friendliness of an Indian village made me feel guilty. I felt incapable of decompressing and just letting life roll on by at the village's measured pace.

Somehow I had conditioned myself to reject the quiet and live in the noisy chaos of the modern world. It wasn't easy for me to unplug and detox from it all. It was as if I was coming off of a drug; a drug of busyness, information, to-do lists, and a brain full of everything I must do.

What's truly amazing is that the pace of my life, and all the distractions vying for my attention, have multiplied tenfold since that quiet day in that quiet place. The battle has only become more intense, and it seems more intense for those around me too. It's as if the world is choking off our ability to live while promising to improve our quality of life. You can see this tension in the tired eyes that surround you at work, at church, in the grocery store, and in the eyes that stare at you out of the mirror at the end of a long day. We are exhausted from trying to keep up, from forcing ourselves into a pace that is neither natural nor healthy.

We live in a time that rewards busyness and expects immediacy. We live in a world rotating so quickly that sparks are flying off in every direction. Just watch how people grab their phones just to make sure someone doesn't need them. Watch how they try and fail to turn off, disconnect, and live independently of the wires that bind us together across the globe. People are finding it increasingly difficult to cut those wires, and even when they try, they usually fail.

Something is badly broken. We've never lived in a more promising time, and yet it seems as though so many people find those promises hollow. Never before has technology so illuminated the prospects of our future, and yet it seems all that is meant to enhance our lives has robbed us of the ability to actually enjoy it. Never before has wealth been so rapidly and easily accrued for so many, and yet it never seems to be satisfying. Never before in history have we had more reasons to feel fulfilled and accomplished, and more things to help us find our way. Never have we had more opportunities to make ourselves happy, and yet never before has emptiness been as painfully obvious as it is in the people we see every day.

The other day I read about a famous person who had accumulated for himself everything he had ever wanted, everything anyone could ever want. He had every reason to live fully, to laugh like those old men in that tiny village, and to be happy. Yet, like so many before him, his life ended in tragedy. Could it be that what we're looking for is what we already have but have long lost the ability to find?

The best way to end this journey together is for you to end it alone. Go to a quiet place with you, your God, and his Book. Ask yourself what has spoken to you most intensely as you've journeyed through *these* pages, and then decide you're going to do something about what you've heard.

God's will isn't hard to find. It's harder to do.

Anyone can dream.

The real dreamers know when to wake up and act.

If you don't, who will play your part in God's story, and fulfill your mission in Jesus' commission?

Jesus is calling down from the heavens, "Get to it!"

I think it's high time we do.

ACKNOWLEDGMENTS

To my dear wife, Andrea, and our little boy, Edward.

And a special thank you to my research team: Melody Stone, Dan Bolton, and Corey Hayes.

Without your help, and without your support, I simply couldn't have done this.

There are no words to express my gratitude.

The best I can do is say "Thank you."

From the bottom of my heart.

APPENDIX

DECISION MAKING AND THE WILL OF GOD

Based upon the work of Dr. Garry Friesen

ALL I HEARD IN SUNDAY SCHOOL GROWING UP WAS how God had a prearranged plan for my life and how I must follow it in order to be a good Christian. I had to be very careful in every decision I made, because if I made one deviation from the plan, my life would spiral wildly out of control. If I missed the mark, I was done. Finished. His plan for me would be thrown away and I would never live up to my potential.

I missed that quiet time before school?

Well that clearly explains why I failed that test . . .

I followed these beliefs growing up because that is

what the church taught me. It was delivered from the pulpit that God "has a life plan for you and you must follow this or you won't amount to anything." Anything but embracing God's "first will" meant taking his second or third best for my life. If I had known then that this approach to God's will was a relatively new theological idea, I would have been saved from much unnecessary pressure and indecision in my life. Instead, after a few missed choices, I was sure that I had wrecked God's road map for my life and I would not amount to anything. I was stuck. My tires were spinning in the mud.

Everyone has, at one point or another, succumbed to this belief. Maybe your experience is similar to mine and you grew up plagued by this anxiety about missing God's best. Maybe you've fallen into the belief that just because you haven't received some miraculous sign from God, you can't move forward with your decision.

You can walk into any Christian bookstore and find mountains of books that apparently give the secret formula to discovering God's will for your life—to hitting the bull's-eye—as if some mad-scientist theologian has concocted the way to always hit God's target.

The point of this book is to argue that there isn't a target to hit.

If you have made a few "second-best" choices and feel as if you struggle with hitting God's right option every time, be relieved. Instead of spending hundreds of dollars on these books or attending conferences set around this relatively contemporary idea, let's take a deeper look into the "way of wisdom" and each principle that was briefly mentioned earlier in chapter five of this book.

1. Where God commands, we must obey.
2. Where there is no command, God gives us freedom (and responsibility) to choose.
3. Where there is no command, God gives us wisdom to choose.
4. When we have chosen what is moral and wise, we must trust the sovereign God to work all the details together for good.

Notice that each point builds on the previous one. For instance, if you don't believe in the first principle, it's highly likely you will not see any value in the second, third, and fourth principle.

1: WHERE GOD COMMANDS, WE MUST OBEY.

THE FIRST POINT IS FAR FROM CONTROVERSIAL. FOR A Christian who takes the Bible seriously, this is not debatable. Plenty of scriptures reinforce the idea that obeying God's commands is foundational to our faith. For instance:

If you love me, you will keep my commandments.
(John 14:15 ESV)

This is how we know that we love the children of
God: by loving God and carrying out his commands.
(1 John 5:2 NIV)

When all has been heard, the conclusion of the matter
is: fear God and keep His commands, because this is
for all humanity. (Eccl. 12:13 HCSB)

Christ himself was not exempt from following the
commands of the Father:

For I have come down from heaven, not to do My own
will, but the will of Him who sent Me. This is the will
of the Father who sent Me, that of all He has given
Me I should lose nothing, but should raise it up at the
last day. And this is the will of Him who sent Me, that
everyone who sees the Son and believes in Him may
have everlasting life; and I will raise him up at the last
day. (John 6:38–40 NKJV)

No matter your subset of Christianity, you will most
likely believe in this principle. Differences start to arise
with the second and third principles found below. These
are the ones that are most challenged and challenging,

and they can, unfortunately, be very divisive to those within the church.

2: WHERE THERE IS NO COMMAND, GOD GIVES US FREEDOM (AND RESPONSIBILITY) TO CHOOSE.

There are two main responses to this second principle. Some see this principle as advocating a form of deism in which God steps back from involvement in the world he has created and leaves things to run on their own. Others rejoice in this because the burden and fear of waiting for divine approval for every decision has been lifted from their shoulders.

While the idea that we are free to choose is certainly a relief in many ways, it also comes with great responsibility; the responsibility of making sure that we are in right relationship with an all-knowing and all-seeing God while making these decisions and that we really are seeking to glorify him in the decision he has authorized us to make for ourselves.

The life of Moses is full of moments where God specifically commands him to do something, but there are also times in the narrative where Moses is responsible to make the right choice of several options. Hebrews 11:24–25 says, "By faith Moses, when he had grown up, refused to be known as the son of Pharaoh's daughter. He chose to be mistreated along with the people of God rather than to enjoy the fleeting pleasures of sin" (NIV). The first few words of this verse are crucial in understanding the life of Moses. He wasn't commanded by God to disregard royalty. On the contrary, the verse begins with, "By faith Moses" and then midway through it notes that "he chose." Moses made his choice; the rest is history.

All throughout the Bible, account after account shows someone faced with a choice. People who choose correctly are celebrated, while those who make the foolish choices are used as an example. We think that God treats us like a micromanaging employer, always looking over our shoulders, commanding us to do this or that in a particular way. Yet that's not how God is at all. He doesn't want you to fast before every test. He isn't going to let you get in a wreck on the way to work because you forgot to do your quiet time. We aren't the jesters in God's court. We don't have to please the King with routines or juggling. He isn't going to send us away when we drop the ball.

On the contrary, he shows us grace abundantly when we make mistakes, and it's upon this truth that we can rest our confidence when we're faced with making a decision that may, or may not, be the right one in the end.

As C. S. Lewis wrote in *The Screwtape Letters*: "[God] wants [Christians] to learn to walk and must therefore take away His hand; and if only the will to walk is really there He is pleased even with their stumbles."

So how does the Christian make choices when there is no command?

3: WHERE THERE IS NO COMMAND, GOD GIVES US WISDOM TO CHOOSE.

———

This principle is directly tied to the first principle because in verses like Ephesians 5:15–16 we see that God commands us to be wise when making decisions: "Be very careful, then, how you live—not as unwise but as wise, making the most of every opportunity, because the days are evil" (NIV). There are many instances in which we are faced with a decision not directly addressed in the Bible. Sometimes these decisions are mundane and insignificant, even though we are presented with two equally good choices. I can order a chocolate milkshake or a vanilla milkshake. Both decisions are a win. Does the rest of life really hang in the balance by the outcome of this decision?

Some decisions, however, require that one exercise great wisdom, and wisdom is often personified in Scripture as being always available, pleading for all to hear her voice. The beginning of Proverbs 8 starts out with, "Doesn't Wisdom call out?" (v. 1), and then a few verses later it says, "People, I call out to you; my cry is to mankind. Learn to be shrewd, you who are inexperienced;

develop common sense, you who are foolish. Listen, for I speak of noble things, and what my lips say is right" (vv. 4–6 HCSB). Wisdom is there; you just have to go for it. You just have to learn to listen to her quiet voice, and push to the side all the other voices that try to convince you to follow other paths.

When the apostle Paul was confronted with a choice about the church in Thessalonica, he wrote that "we thought it best" (1 Thess. 3:1 NIV) to depart from the church and send Timothy to them instead. Paul didn't write that he didn't make a decision until God gave him a sign but instead implied that he relied on his abilities because he "thought it best." This same way of decision making is featured numerous times in the early church: "I considered it necessary" (Phil. 2:25–26 NKJV); "it is not desirable" (Acts 6:2–4 NKJV); "I have decided" (Titus 3:12). These decisions weren't prearranged by God's will. The disciples had the freedom to act and make choices based upon wisdom, and so they did.

4: WHEN WE HAVE CHOSEN WHAT IS MORAL AND WISE, WE MUST TRUST THE SOVEREIGN GOD TO WORK ALL THE DETAILS TOGETHER FOR GOOD.

If we know of God's commands, why do we keep offering him a deal when faced with a fork in the road? *Lord, do this so I will know to do that and such. Lord, I know you want me to graduate college, so help me with this exam.* What we are asking is for the God of the universe to reveal himself in a special way at a special time preferred by us. We pray all these things, expecting a sign, and when it does not come, we are left feeling dejected.

Prayer should not be our attempt to bend God's will to fit our schedule or preferences. You might say: "But Gideon did this! Gideon asked God to reveal his will in Judges 6! I can show you in my Bible!" Yes, there are times recorded in the Bible when God audibly spoke and performed miracles. The recipients clearly understood him. They were given a straightforward plan and expected to follow it. God was very specific in these instances, and one of these times is found in the story of Gideon. He asked God to prove himself and, sure enough, God followed through. You have to wonder, though, is our situation like Gideon's? Should all believers expect the response from God when there is a difficult decision ahead just because of Gideon's instance?

The answer to both of these questions is a firm no. Gideon was a judge, who had been called by God for a specific purpose and moment. Besides, he is not honored in Scripture for his decision to test God; on the contrary, his hesitation and cowardice robbed him of the chance to bring honor on himself by killing the leader of his enemies, who was instead delivered into the hands of a woman named Jael.

The wisdom view accounts for these various instances in Scripture. Occasionally, God directly guides an individual, but when he does this, it is through an angelic encounter, burning bush, or dazzling light, not a fluttering of the heart. You see these people who experience God's revelation as immediately knowing they were dealing with God, without a doubt. They hear his voice and are certain; there is no misunderstanding. If you are questioning if God has spoken to you, don't worry, there is no question when he speaks. You couldn't question it if you tried.

Also, you might ask, "Is laying out a fleece, as Gideon did, right?" How often have we set out our metaphorical fleeces in hopes of a sign that meets all of our prearranged specifications? We test God by sending up "If you do this, I will do this" prayers. We look for God's will and expect confirmation to be the brandishing of supernatural power. Our situation isn't Gideon's, and God's response to Gideon will not be his response to us. Instead, see your fleece for what it really is: an emotional ploy, an attempt to manipulate God. We try to put God in an either/or situation when he has already told us what to do.

One of the most quoted verses in opposition to this view is Proverbs 16:9: "The mind of man plans his way, but the LORD directs his steps" (NASB). You have most likely heard it paraphrased as, "Man tries to do his own thing but God directs everything." This paraphrase assumes that it is talking about God's moral will or individual will when in reality it is talking about his sovereign will. This proverb is not restricted to the Christian only, but to all men. God wins. We plan out our days and we live our lives, but God's sovereign will always prevails. His will takes into account all of our individual decisions, and it is not derailed by the exercise of our personal freedom.

The way of wisdom does not argue against the authority of God's sovereign will. Man is free to plan and scheme, but ultimately, God determines the direction. German theologian Franz Delitzsch summed it up quite well by saying when a man understands that God's sovereign will ultimately prevails, he should "do his duty and leave the rest, with humility and confidence, to God." Dr. Delitzsch is absolutely correct.

We see in Romans 1:11–13 and 15:24 where Paul planned out his schedule to meet with churches and believers. He said that he had often "planned to come to you" (1:13 NKJV) and, "I plan to do so when I go to Spain" (15:24 NIV). Planning isn't bad, and in your planning you can rest assured that God hasn't taken his hands off the steering wheel. So perhaps it's time to stop asking, "How do I find the will of God?" and start asking, "How do I make good decisions?" Scripture compels us to do God's will rather than find it.

A SUMMARY

———

You can remember the principles presented in Dr. Friesen's book *Decision Making and the Will of God* by thinking of four words: *obedience, freedom, wisdom,* and *trust.*

When God commands, we have to be *obedient.* When God does not explicitly command something in Scripture and we are left with a grey area, God gives us *freedom* to figure it out. If there isn't a commandment and we are left with the freedom to choose, God gives us *wisdom* and we must rely on wisdom to make good choices. And finally, when we have done our part—that is, when we have exercised our freedom and made the wise choice—we have to *trust* that he ultimately works "for the good of those who love him" (Rom. 8:28 NIV).

FURTHER READING

———

- *How Then Should We Choose? Three Views on God's Will and Decision Making* by Douglas Huffman
- *Guidance: What the Bible Says About Knowing God's Will* by Oliver Barclay

- *Decision Making God's Way: A New Model for Knowing God's Will* by Gary Meadors
- *Decisions, Decisions: How (and How Not) to Make Them* by Dave Swavely
- *Decision Making by the Book: How to Choose Wisely in an Age of Options* by Haddon W. Robinson

NOTES

CHAPTER 1

1. Brother Andrew with Susan DeVore Williams, *And God Changed His Mind* (Ada, MI: Chosen Books, 1990), 35–36.
2. Antonio Spadaro, S.J., "A Big Heart Open to God: The exclusive interview with Pope Francis," *America: The National Catholic Review*, September 30, 2013, http://www.americamagazine.org/pope-interview.

CHAPTER 2

1. F. F. Bruce, *Paul: Apostle of the Heart Set Free* (Colorado Springs, CO: Eerdmans, 2000), 34–35.
2. Ibid., 51.
3. Everett Ferguson, *Backgrounds in Early Christianity* (Colorado Springs, CO: Eerdmans, 2003).

4. Bill Adler Sr., *Ask Billy Graham: The World's Best-Loved Preacher Answers Your Most Important Questions* (Nashville: Thomas Nelson, 2007), 77.
5. David D. Lee, *Sergeant York: An American Hero* (Lexington, Kentucky: The University Press of Kentucky, 2002).
6. Erik Rees, *S.H.A.P.E.: Finding and Fulfilling Your Unique Purpose for Life* (Grand Rapids: Zondervan, 2006).

CHAPTER 3

1. Katie Davis with Beth Clark, *Kisses from Katie: A Story of Relentless Love and Redemption* (Brentwood, TN: Howard Books, 2012).
2. Ibid.

CHAPTER 4

1. John Piper, "Unreached Peoples: The Unique and Primary Goal of Missions," Desiringgod.org, January 1, 1991, www.desiringgod.org/resource-library/articles /unreached-peoples.
2. Richard Stearns, *Unfinished: Believing Is Only the Beginning* (Nashville: Thomas Nelson, 2013), xix.
3. Phillip K. Freeman, *Alexander the Great* (New York: Simon & Schuster, 2011). http://www.ancient.eu.com /article/94/.

CHAPTER 5

1. Garry Friesen and J. Robin Maxson, *Decision Making and the Will of God: A Biblical Alternative to the Traditional View* (Colorado Springs, CO: Multnomah, 2004), 421.

CHAPTER 6

1. Martin Rinkart, "Now Thank We All Our God," circa 1636. Public domain.
2. David. W. Koeller, "Julian the Apostate: Letter to

Arsacius," accessed January 27, 2014, http://www
.thenagain.info/classes/sources/julian.html.

3. C. S. Lewis, *The Screwtape Letters* (New York:
Macmillian, 1950), 143–45.

CHAPTER 8

1. http://www.forbes.com/sites/jeannemeister/2012/10/05
/millennialmindse/.

2. Brian Monahan, *God's Bestseller: William Tyndale,
Thomas More, and The Writing of the English Bible—A
Story of Martyrdom and Betrayal* (New York: St. Martin's
Press, 2003); http://library.osu.edu/innovation-projects
/omeka/exhibits/show/the-king-james-bible/sections/item
/15.

3. C. S. Lewis, *Mere Christianity* (San Francisco: Harper
San Francisco, 2009), 87.

CHAPTER 9

1. Anne Isba, *The Excellent Mrs. Fry: Unlikely Heroine*
(London: Continuum, 2010); http://www.nwhm.org
/education-resources/biography/biographies/elizabeth-fry/.

CHAPTER 10

1. John P. Meyer and Natalie J. Allen, *Commitment in the
Workplace* (Thousand Oaks, CA: SAGE Publications), 1997.

2. http://www.britannica.com/EBchecked/topic/120070
/Thomas-Clarkson.

3. BBC, "Historic Figures: Florence Nightingale (1820–
1910)," accessed January 29, 2014, http://www.bbc.co.uk
/history/historic_figures/nightingale_florence.shtml.

4. A+E Networks, "Florence Nightingale," accessed January
29, 2014, http://www.biography.com/people/florence
-nightingale-9423539?page=2.

5. Christopher Gill and Gillian Gill, "Nightingale in

Scutari: Her Legacy Reexamined," Abstract, *Clinical Infectious Diseases* (2005) 40 (12): 1799-1805. doi: 10.1086/430380, http://cid.oxfordjournals.org/content /40/12/1799.full.

6. *Encyclopedia Britannica,* s. v. "Florence Nightingale," accessed January 29, 2014, http://www.britannica.com /EBchecked/topic/415020/Florence-Nightingale.

7. http://www.familylife.com/articles/topics/marriage/staying -married/commitment/the-true-story-behind-the-vow#. UwTl5xAqu-U.

8. C. S. Lewis, *God in the Dock* (Grand Rapids, MI: Eerdmans: 1970), 49.

9. Corrie ten Boom House Foundation, "History," accessed January 29, 2014, http://www.corrietenboom.com/history .htm.

10. United States Holocaust Memorial Museum, "Holocaust Encyclopedia, s. v. 'Corrie ten Boom,'" accessed January 29, 2014, http://www.ushmm.org/wlc/en/article.php ?ModuleId=10006914.

11. Corrie ten Boom, *The Hiding Place* (Peabody, MA: Hendrickson Publishers, 2006), 240.

12. The University of Alabama in Huntsville, "Corrie ten Boom," accessed January 29, 2014, http://webpages.uah .edu/~bnf0001/webpage2.html.

13. Yad Vashem (The Holocaust Martyrs' and Heroes' Remembrance Authority), "The Righteous Among the Nations: s. v. 'Boom ten Cornelia (1892–1983),'" accessed January 29, 2014, http://db.yadvashem.org /righteous/righteousName.html?language=en&ite mId=4014036.

CHAPTER 11

1. http://www.wdm.ca/artifact_articles/bedaux.htm; http://royalbcmuseum.bc.ca/assets/Bedaux_Expedition .pdf.

CHAPTER 12

1. Mark Driscoll, "7 Things I've Learned from Dr. John Piper," accessed January 29, 2014, http://theresurgence.com/2013/04/17/7-things-i-ve-learned-from-dr-john-piper.

2. http://people.bridgewater.edu/~atrupe/ENG140/quotations_WhyWrite.htm.

CHAPTER 14

1. Ed. Dagobart D. Runes, *The Diary and Sundry Observations of Thomas Alva Edison*.

2. Spoken statement. Published in *Harper's Monthly* in September 1932.

3. http://www.forbes.com/sites/nathanfurr/2011/06/09/how-failure-taught-edison-to-repeatedly-innovate/.

4. Bryan Walsh, "The Electrifying Edison," *Time*, June 23, 2010, http://www.time.com/time/specials/packages/article/0,28804,1999143_1999200_1999163,00.html.

5. Ibid.

CHAPTER 15

1. "Selman A. Waksman–Biographical," Nobelprize.org, accessed February 3, 2014, http://www.nobelprize.org/nobel_prizes/medicine/laureates/1952/waksman-bio.html.

2. Nicole Kresge, Robert D. Simoni, and Robert L. Hill, "Selman Waksman: the Father of Antibiotics," *The Journal of Biological Chemistry*, 279, e7, November 26, 2004, http://www.jbc.org/content/279/48/e7.

3. *Encyclopedia Britannica Online*, s. v. "streptomycin," accessed February 3, 2014, http://www.britannica.com/EBchecked/topic/568848/streptomycin.

4. Harvard University Library Open Collections Program, "Tuberculosis in Europe and North America,

1800–1922," accessed February 3, 2014, http://ocp.hul.
harvard.edu/contagion/tuberculosis.html.

5. The Salvation Army, "Founders William & Catherine
Booth," accessed February 3, 2014, http://salvos.org.au
/about-us/our-history/william-and-catherine-booth.php.

6. Tejvan Pettinger, "Biography William Booth," February
13, 2013, http://www.biographyonline.net/spiritual/
william-booth.html.

7. http://www.salvationarmyusa.org/usn/history-of-the
-salvation-army.

8. https://s3.amazonaws.com/usn-cache.salvationarmy.org
/7f4d4f3c-c6df-42f5-a74b-ed7f2591085b_Service+Stats
+16.pdf.

9. The Salvation Army of Palm Beach County, Florida,
"Founder–William Booth," accessed February 3, 2014,
http://www.uss.salvationarmy.org/uss/www_uss
_westpalmbeach.nsfvw-print/309032CE20B6C01985257
5BE00754199?openDocument.

10. Harry Ricketts, *Rudyard Kipling: A Life* (New York: Carol
& Graf, 1999), 184.

ABOUT THE AUTHOR

JOHNNIE MOORE SERVED FOR A DOZEN YEARS AT Liberty University as the university's campus pastor and senior vice president. He now works as chief of staff to film and television producer, Mark Burnett.

He serves on the boards of World Help, the National Association of Evangelicals, and on the U.S. Lausanne Committee. He has written regularly for international media outlets like CNN, Fox News, and the *Washington Post*, and he has been cited in every major media outlet in America.

He has worked with governments, churches, and NGOs in more than two dozen nations, affecting change in some of the world's most desperate and difficult places. He is also one of America's best-known advocates for international religious freedom.

Moore has been named by PR News as one of America's top young PR executives, *Christianity Today* has designated him a "who's next" leader of the next generation of evangelicals, and his work as a messaging consultant garnered a major front-page profile in the *Washington Post*. Moore is also the founder of a boutique public relations firm, The Kairos Company, which helps faith-based and secular organizations communicate more clearly when things are going well, and when they aren't.

He lives near Santa Monica with his wife, Andrea, and their children.

WWW.JOHNNIEMOORE.ORG

TWITTER: @JOHNNIEM

FACEBOOK: FACEBOOK.COM/JOHNNIEONLINE

WWW.WORLDHELP.NET